NOVEL
AND
READER

JOHN FLETCHER

MARION BOYARS
LONDON : BOSTON

First Published in Great Britain and the United States in 1980
By Marion Boyars Publishers Ltd.
18 Brewer Street, London W1R 4AS.
and Marion Boyars Publishers Inc.
99 Main Street, Salem, New Hampshire 03079

Australian distribution by Thomas C. Lothian
4-12 Tattersalls Lane, Melbourne, Victoria 3000.

© John Fletcher 1980

British Library Cataloguing in Publication Data
Fletcher, John, *b. 1937*
Novel and reader.
1. Fiction—19th century—History and criticism
2. Fiction—20th century—History and criticism
1. Title
809.3'3   PN3499

Library of Congress Catalog Card No. 79-56842

ISBN 0 7145 2620 7   Hardcover edition

Printed and bound in Great Britain by
Redwood Burn Limited
Trowbridge & Esher

CONTENTS

I, peasantly pig-eyed
Mark the wet frith
Once my people ploughed
And at the agent's invitation
Inspect their cottages, all mod con
Three knocked together into one
Where they jostled, stooped and lied

JONATHAN FUNE

PREFACE AND ACKNOWLEDGEMENTS

Io non posso ritrar di tutti appieno:
però che si mi caccia il lungo tema,
che molte volte al fatto il dir vien meno.
                DANTE

'It was the devotion and drive of his heart toward that yearning crowd
that made him skilful in his art', writes Felix Krull, in Thomas Mann's
last great fictional portrait of the artist; 'if he bestows on them joy of
life and they satiate him with their applause for doing so, is not that a
mutual fulfilment, a meeting and marriage of his yearning and theirs?'
My book deals with the relationship between the writer of fiction and
his audience, and with the satisfactions—of every kind—which novels
afford us. Indeed, if Roland Barthes had not already used the phrase
plaisir du texte—understood in the widest sense, as enrichment and
delight from products of the human imagination—it would have
suited my purpose exactly. My chief concern is with the humane
qualities in literature and with the social dimension of fiction; for in
using the very term 'fiction', I would wish to be understood to mean
something broader than simply the novel and the short story, though I
would not extend the definition of the word as far as, say, Frank
Kermode does in *The Sense of an Ending*, or as Wallace Stevens does
in his poem 'Notes Toward a Supreme Fiction'. The term as I use it
relates more closely to 'story' than to 'poesis', but certainly involves
more than 'plot' or 'narrative'.

As I am looking for patterns, themes and motifs in an elusive, rich
and varied aesthetic form, the method I adopt is a cumulative one,
working inwards from a number of complementary angles. The first
chapter is introductory, and analyzes the way in which the basic form
of European fiction was consolidated around 1830—at the same time
as the 'parvenu' hero came to prominence—in such novels as
Stendhal's *Scarlet and Black*. The next chapter deals with the
'involuted' fictional forms characteristic of turn-of-the-century
Modernism, especially in the novels of Proust, Joyce and Thomas
Mann. The third demonstrates how fiction persuades and even cajoles
us into accepting a particular point of view, and the fourth discusses

how a key novel explores extreme situations. The subject of the fifth chapter is psychological fiction; women's writing is examined in chapter six and Europe's mythical view of America in chapter seven. The eighth chapter offers some general conclusions arising from the preceding discussion, and stresses the closeness of the relationship between writer and reader, between novels and the people to whom they are addressed.

My approach is therefore sometimes broad, synthetic, allusive; sometimes it is more minute, even closely textual. None of the novels or other works I discuss is unfamiliar to the average reader, I think, at least not in general outline. For that reason I have provided no bibliography other than a short listing of major secondary works mentioned in the text; any up-to-date paperback catalogue will supply details about available editions of the novels which I discuss. For similar reasons of brevity and convenience quotations (identified at first mention) are given in English, the translation being my own unless otherwise acknowledged, and titles are also given in English, in the usually received British form (e.g. *The Outsider* rather than *The Stranger,* and *Scarlet and Black* rather than *The Red and the Black;* key examples like this tend to be taken from French literature, for reasons explained in the first chapter).

Although I consider my tastes in fiction reasonably catholic, I could not have concealed my likes and dislikes even if I had wanted to. Some of my judgements are not uncontroversial, for instance that *The Outsider* is Camus's only great novel, or that Alain-Fournier's *Le Grand Meaulnes* is over-rated. But I hope I am not guilty of prejudice, and that when the reader comes to the end of the book he will find it has helped him to a greater understanding of the art of the novel, that most attractive and at the same time most bewildering of forms invented by the restless genius of man.

Like most of my writing, this study has arisen out of the active teaching situation in which as a university professor I am constantly engaged. It is thus a particular pleasure to acknowledge the profit gained from discussions with successive generations of students at the universities of Durham, East Anglia, Odense, Salzburg, Konstanz and Yaoundé, especially Anne-Marie Bülow-Møller, Robert Burden, Hannelore Fahrenbach and Tricia Sharpe, and with many colleagues and former colleagues, among them Malcolm Bradbury, Thomas

PREFACE AND ACKNOWLEDGEMENTS

Elsässer, Eric Homberger, Wolfgang Iser, Brian Rowley, Robert Stuart Short, Jay Silverman and Peter Whyte. All of them have left their mark on the book in ways they may not always recognize, even less approve, but for which I am grateful. I have not however been influenced only by my academic environment; I have benefited from contacts with practising novelists as different as Samuel Beckett, Malcolm Bradbury, Margaret Drabble, Wilson Harris, Franz Innerhofer, Claude Simon and Angus Wilson. Finally, I owe more than I can precisely say to my former headmaster, Denys Thompson, who first showed me how to read with discernment.

As the book has been several years in the making, parts of it have already appeared in unrevised and often rather different form in the following publications, to which acknowledgement is gratefully made: *Comparative Literature Studies; Critical Quarterly; A Dictionary of Modern Critical Terms* (ed. Roger Fowler); *The French Review; The International Fiction Review; Modernism 1890-1930* (ed. Malcolm Bradbury and James McFarlane); *Samuel Beckett Now* (ed. Melvin J. Friedman); and *The Spectator*.

I have indicated clearly at first mention sources of short quotations from novels and other works not in the public domain and make grateful acknowledgement to the copyright holders specified.

John Fletcher

CHAPTER ONE

Parvenu Genre,
Genre of Parvenus

CHAPTER ONE

Parvenu Genre, Genre of Parvenus

Novels have beginnings, ends, and
potentiality, even if the world has not.

FRANK KERMODE

I

'Introductions'—Ian Watt wittily remarks somewhere—'begin by
being infinitely expandable and end by proving equally expendable.'
This introductory chapter, too, could go on for a long time, especially
in that it is concerned with a major figure in European fiction, the
provincial upstart, who emerges into full maturity simultaneously
with the genre itself. So in order to keep the discussion within
reasonable bounds, I propose anchoring it around one major novel, to
which I shall relate a number of others. It happens that this is a French
book; the same will frequently be the case as well in the chapters which
follow. This is because the novel, the most all-embracing genre which
literary art has evolved—protean in its shape, broad in its sweep,
profound in its quest—has attained its most perfect form in France.
Other nations have no doubt produced greater novels—*Moby Dick*,
Anna Karenina and *Little Dorrit* have no serious rivals anywhere—but
in few other literatures has the art of fiction been developed to such a
pitch of exactness and skill; perhaps because, as Albert Camus once
said, the French novel incorporates 'a certain conception of man',
relies on 'marvellous economy', and shows 'passionate monotony' in
its aspiration towards balanced rigour and shape: for to be classical, he
maintained, one must know how to repeat oneself. Drieu La Rochelle,
for his part, defined the French novel in these terms: 'A unilinear,
egocentric narrative, fairly narrowly humanistic to the point of
seeming abstract, not very profuse'. As a result the subtleties of the
French novel tend to be those which appear at once, on the surface: they
are above all psychological and rational qualities. Those of the greatest

13

English and Russian novels are more subterranean. The French novel—tragic, ethical and trim—can thus show greater polish and stylishness, but not often the rugged, sometimes imperfect grandeur of the finest novels written in other languages. Outside France there may be no precise equivalent for *The Princess of Cleves, Dangerous Liaisons, Sentimental Education* or *Man's Estate,* let alone for a host of minor French masterpieces like *Adolphe* or *Strait is the Gate;* but neither can French literature boast a *Brothers Karamazov* or a *Women in Love.*

This study begins, nevertheless, with a French work, the earliest of the great nineteenth-century novels, the first complex and multifaceted fiction:*Scarlet and Black.* All previous novels—even those of Cervantes, Fielding, Laclos and Jane Austen—lack at least one dimension. *Don Quixote* may be robust, but it can be crude and primitive, *Tom Jones* is exquisite but implausible, *Dangerous Liaisons* is brilliant but narrowly-focused, *Pride and Prejudice* is wise, urbane but socially and historically limited: and here I am speaking only about the very greatest works produced in the first couple of centuries of the novel's development, not of fascinating curiosities or indispensable landmarks like *Tristram Shandy* and *Robinson Crusoe.* I am talking of the central tradition of the novel in Europe: and in that tradition, *Scarlet and Black* is the first major undisputed masterpiece. But Stendhal could not have published his psychological *chef-d'oeuvre* in 1831 without this rich and diverse literary heritage behind him; nor—as Ian Watt points out, at the end of his classic study *The Rise of the Novel*—could either he or Balzac have attained the greatness they did if social changes following upon the French Revolution had not created a critical climate which was much more favourable to the development of formal realism than was that of neo-classicism, for neo-classical aesthetics limited the achievement of novelists prior to Stendhal, whatever their individual stature.

II

Although not a neo-classical work, *Scarlet and Black* is, for all that, a novel which looks backward as much as forward. To take an obvious example, it looks forward in the kind of colour symbolism which permeates the whole book, from the very title onwards. It is well known that 'scarlet' represents military glory, and 'black' represents a clerical career. In restoration France the profession of arms is closed to Julien Sorel, and the church alone lies open to him. This is made

explicit on a number of occasions, not least after he has received a
declaration of love from Mathilde: 'I, a poor peasant from the Jura', he
keeps repeating to himself, 'I, who am condemned to wear this dreary
black coat year in, year out! Alas, twenty years earlier I'd have been in
uniform like them!' He is thinking here of Mathilde's friends, many of
whom are young officers. 'In those days a man of my salt', he realizes,
'was either killed, or *a General at thirty-six*' (Penguin Classics ed., p.
334). Of course, Julien is aware of being more intelligent than the
young noblemen of his acquaintance, since, as he puts it, he knows how
to 'choose the uniform of the day'. *That* uniform is the black cassock of
the priest: the man who is able by intrigue and insinuation to rise to the
highest places in the land. Since the fall of Napoleon, Julien realizes
with regret, military glory has ceased to be available to a young man of
humble origins, even to matter very much at all.

Colour symbolism is less pervasively but just as effectively
employed in the distinction which the Marquis, Julien's employer,
establishes between the 'man in black' and the 'man in blue.' Julien, as
the Marquis's secretary, wears black during the daytime in order to
execute with proper sobriety his functions as his Lordship's servant
and officer, but is given a blue suit to wear in the drawing room in the
evenings. This effectively creates two different personalities, and
Julien delights the Marquis by his tact in showing his awareness that
the distinction must be maintained in all their relations. 'Will your
Lordship graciously permit me to decline this gift?' he asks at one
point. 'It is not addressed to the man in black, and it would entirely
spoil the relations you have so kindly allowed to exist with the man in
blue' (p. 289). So impressed is the Marquis with this delicacy—for
Julien's behaviour is dignified and even 'aristocratic'—he determines
henceforward to treat him as nobly born. Such subtle uses of colour
symbolism are original in Stendhal, and become commonplace only
later in the history of the novel.

Another and more striking example of Stendhal's artistic foresight is
his study of the ups and downs of love, which goes beyond the
titillating libertinism common in the eighteenth century. In fact, he
shows an almost modern awareness of sexual psychology; in his essay
On Love he discusses what he calls the fiasco: 'The first triumph', he
writes, 'is very often a painful effort', and he demonstrates this in
action in *Scarlet and Black,* where both Julien's love affairs start off
with the participants not experiencing quite the delirium they had
expected or indeed promised themselves. Except for Madame de

Rênal, in fact, they all go in for love more as an effort of will than as a result of overwhelming passion: Julien seduces his first employer's wife because he feels he owes it to his pride to do so, and Mathilde, the Marquis's daughter, gives herself to Julien later because she believes she is thereby acting in the style of her noble ancestors. True love is born only some time after these rather forced transports: Stendhal was as lucid as Marcel Proust about the way love operates in the human heart. It is Proust who writes that in love there is perpetual suffering, which joy renders virtual, neutralizes, postpones, but which can become unbearable at any moment, as it would indeed have been all along, if one had not been successful in initially getting one's way with the loved one. Thus the fruits of love are continually being poisoned by the act of loving itself; there is nothing permanent in love, Proust argues, for we are always in danger of suffering even at those moments when we are happiest.

Such opinions would have been shared by Stendhal. He demonstrates in masterly detail how it is jealousy which reveals to the innocent lover the fact that he or she is in love: 'Seated on a chair in the antechamber of these rooms, Madame de Rênal fell a prey to all the horrors of jealousy. Her utter lack of experience served her again at this moment—amazement tempered her grief' (p. 77). Mathilde, as a young lady living in the metropolis and an ardent reader of novels, finds out much more quickly that she is in love: 'She ran over in her mind', Stendhal tells us, 'all the descriptions of passion she had read of in *Manon Lescaut,* the *Nouvelle Héloïse,* the *Lettres d'une religieuse portugaise,* and so forth' (p. 321). His analysis of Mathilde in love is particularly incisive: she falls in love with Julien, he suggests, in order to escape her boredom; once she has become his mistress, she stops feeling bored, and so without in the least suspecting it Julien loses at a stroke his greatest advantage over her. He on the other hand finds everything changed in his heart from the moment he thinks that he has quarrelled with her for ever. Mathilde, sure of being loved, feels, we are told, nothing but contempt for Julien, while Julien suffers the torments of the damned as a spurned lover. It is only by working in his turn upon her jealousy and love that he is able to destroy her pride; but in the process he must keep an inhuman grip upon his own emotions and especially his longing to seize her in his arms and beg her forgiveness. He finally 'brings her to heel' (the metaphor, though crude, is not inappropriate in the circumstances) by paying assiduous court to and pretending that he is in love with someone else. He wins the day only by superior self-command; but what a terrible price to pay in a love affair like this!

But Stendhal's subtlety and acuteness go even further. He uses the psychology of love to point up an essential difference between the two women in the novel. The fact that Mathilde does not commit herself to Julien by repeating the experience of their first night of love on subsequent nights not only distinguishes her from Madame de Rênal, but also prepares for the dénouement, in which her actions will be dictated more by pride, and a consciousness of what she owes to her position as an aristocratic mistress, than by any genuine devotion to Julien himself. The behaviour of the two women at the very end is characteristic: Mathilde drives to the burial with her lover's head on her lap in sixteenth-century style, whereas Madame de Rênal is faithful to her promise neither to survive Julien nor to commit suicide: 'Madame de Rênal did not attempt in any way to take her own life; but, three days after Julien's death', we are told, 'she gave her children a last embrace and died' (p. 509). The two women are different even in the manner in which they respond to jealousy: jealousy makes Mathilde yield totally to Julien, whereas the same emotion reveals to Madame de Rênal the full extent of her love for him; it indicates in other words the essential selfishness of the one, and the utter selflessness of the other. It can hardly be over-emphasized how subtle Stendhal's methods are in establishing the fundamental differences between the two: and it is all done by psychological analysis of the reactions of the protagonists.

Stendhal also looks forward to later developments in fiction in his attitude to the alienation of the hero; this has almost existentialist overtones *avant la lettre*. Early in the book Father Pirard sees in Julien 'something that offends the common run of men' (p. 210); and elsewhere it is stated that Julien is almost literally at war with society. In this he closely resembles Camus's Meursault, whom we shall meet again later in this study. Like Meursault, he gives offence by feeling no tender emotion towards his family, in this case his widowed father: Fouqué, we are told, 'thought he understood why so many people felt a passionate hatred of his friend', because Julien's horror at the idea of seeing his father shocks the honest timber merchant profoundly. Like Meursault, too, Julien refuses to defend himself in a law court: 'It was murder, and premeditated murder,' he concedes to magistrate and counsel alike, 'I'm sorry, gentlemen, but this reduces your task to a very small matter' (p. 476). Camus was undoubtedly thinking of Julien's refusal to take part in the charade of legal defence and its spurious rhetorics—a matter I shall return to later—in his own novel *The Outsider*. But like Meursault Julien is unable to maintain his ruggedly heroic attitude for long; we are told that he found himself moved to self-pity 'like any other faint-hearted human being', but he takes good care, as does Meursault in similar circumstances, not to betray this weakness to anyone. Stendhal seems thus to have grasped with astonishing artistic foresight the essential meaning of the absurd, how the approach of death makes a man lose interest in so much that obsessed him in life: Julien is struck, for instance, by the fact that Mathilde, whom he adored two months previously, now leaves him cold. Again, curiously like Meursault, Julien is approached by a priest in the condemned cell and is begged to repent. His reply is worthy of Meursault's tirade in the same circumstances: 'And what shall I have left', he answers the priest, 'if I despise myself? I have been ambitious, I am not going to blame myself for that; I acted then in accordance with the demands of the time. Now I live for the day, without thought of the morrow' (p. 507).

Stendhal also foreshadows the modern in his 'political atheism' (to borrow a phrase by René Girard). But this links the novel just as readily with eighteenth-century scepticism. Stendhal was a great admirer of earlier writers like Laclos and Voltaire. He is quite as shrewd as Laclos about the motives and methods men employ in seducing women; for example, on a return trip to Madame de Rênal, who is now sunk in religious remorse, Julien manages, by the never-failing device of pretending that he is leaving for ever, to break down her carefully erected defences. But Stendhal, like Laclos, knows that this is not necessarily the path to the highest joy: 'Thus', he informs us, 'after three hours' conversation, Julien obtained what he had so passionately longed for during the first two hours of it. Had a return to tenderness and a forgetfulness of remorse come sooner to Madame de Rênal it would have been the divinest happiness, but contrived in this way by artful means it was merely a pleasure' (p. 233). That is why—as Laclos well knew—'donjuanism' is the mark not of the sensual voluptuary, but of the cerebral chess-player. The influence of Voltaire is more diffuse, but his name is mentioned in *Scarlet and Black* several times, and always with respect, and is commonly used as a stick with which to belabour the reactionaries whom Julien comes across in his career.

But much as Stendhal looked back to the eighteenth century—which was in many ways his true spiritual home—he was still affected by the atmosphere of the Romantic movement in the midst of which he was living at the time. He loves cloak-and-dagger melodrama just like Dickens or Victor Hugo; the one noticeable weakness of the novel, in fact, is the conspiracy section, during which Julien is sent on a secret diplomatic mission and Stendhal indulges his taste for swashbuckling to a quite extraordinary romantic extent. Even the constant stress on alienation—in remarks like 'I see a new something that offends the common run of men' (p. 210)—is in truth more romantic than existentialist. Julien is another symbol of the alienated artist, the Chatterton-figure who obsessed contemporaries as the suffering *enfant du siècle*. Moreover, Julien's romanticism—and Stendhal's through him—is revealed by the fact that he knows much of the *Nouvelle Héloïse* by heart. Although he uses Rousseau's passionate phrases for purposes of which their author would hardly approve, the very fact that he has mastered them reveals considerable respect and admiration. Stendhal's debt to the romantic hero has been well put by Jean-Jacques Mayoux: 'Absurd man', he writes, 'absurd destiny, such throughout is the destiny of Julien, the most sublime representative, in the romantic novel, of the true *mal du siècle*'.

Stendhal was not being immodest, in fact, when he subtitled his novel 'A Chronicle of the Nineteenth Century'; in this it bears comparison—once allowance is made for its smaller compass—with *War and Peace*. He paints a magnificent portait of the society of the period, and deals with a considerable variety of social types (more so, indeed, than Dickens does). Since Julien's origins are humble, we are accorded a glimpse into the world of the richer peasantry (his father is a sawyer); we also look into the homes of the provincial gentry (the Rênals) and of the new parvenu middle class (the Valenods); we see, too, what life was like in a provincial seminary, and also in a great mansion in Paris, the Hôtel de la Mole. Furthermore, the world of political intrigue and ecclesiastical chicanery is laid bare before us, for hardly any form of public corruption remains unexamined; but of all the aspects of contemporary vice which he exposes, Stendhal disapproves most strongly of members of the rising bourgeoisie like Valenod, who having profited from the purchase of church lands were ousting the old landed gentry represented by the Rênals. There is no limit to Stendhal's detestation of the Valenod breed: some of the strongest passages in the book are those which describe their greed, their vulgarity, their coarseness, their crass indifference to either charity or decorum or elegance, and their willingness to stoop to anything in order to further their interests. It is Valenod who finally destroys Julien, not Monsieur de Rênal, who had a great deal more to punish him for. Stendhal's attitude—understandably—is that for all their pride and narrowness of vision, the Rênals of this world are the true aristocracy and deserve the position which the Valenods are busily undermining with a cunning which Lampedusa, a novelist much influenced by Stendhal, has more recently analysed in his Sicilian novel *The Leopard*. Stendhal is also sympathetic to the higher nobility, the princes of the blood, as represented by the proud and fascinating Mathilde. Not that he has any illusions about their limitations: the novel demonstrates that the sixteenth-century values by which Mathilde lives are even more quaint and archaic than Julien's nostalgia for the days of Bonaparte. But at least she—and the Marquis her father—hold to an ideal, and a noble one at that, whereas the Valenods of that world would not hesitate to repudiate their wives for a *préfecture* or sell their daughters for a decoration.

Julien's attitude to the very lowest orders is, however, as ambivalent as his attitude to the aristocracy. He feels contempt for their swinish ways and habits, but is moved to pity at the thought that for people who have experienced starvation on a monotonously regular basis it is hardly surprising 'if in their eyes the happy man is first and foremost one who has just dined well, and next to him the man who owns a good suit of clothes' (p. 197). A similar nervous ambivalence is detectable in Stendhal's attitude to the provinces, which in some contexts he berates for their petty-mindedness and for the tyranny public opinion exercises there, while in other passages he rhapsodizes about the naturalness of life far from Paris. Much of the book's charm comes from these ambiguities, which represent a good deal more than mere vulgar inconsistency, constituting instead fruitful tensions of attitude.

This ambivalence is particularly marked in Stendhal's stance towards Julien. There is evidently an element of wish-fulfilment in the sexual conquest of Madame de Rênal and Mathilde; but although in this, as in other ways, too, Stendhal reveals his involvement with his hero, he is not uncritical. What we are offered, in fact, is a portrait in the round of a likeable but impulsive young man who is basically honourable in spite of his boundless ambition, and who is destroyed because he habitually follows the dictates of his wounded integrity rather than the mean calculations of prudence. Even at the last he throws all caution to the winds, and by speaking his mind in his address to the jury renders null all efforts to have him acquitted. His conduct is seen by others as a kind of suicide; but it is the last and the noblest expression of his fundamental decency, and his apparent failure in court constitutes in fact his greatest success. He is unwilling to go on playing the game which society forces upon him: had he been born noble and rich, he would have been able to exercise his talents without petty compromise; he could have cut a figure not unlike that of the Marquis de la Mole whom he so greatly admires and respects. As it is, his brains are his only asset; and to turn them effectively to account he would have to emulate the insinuating guile of the Abbé de Frilair. But such devious conduct, such inhuman self-control, such distortion of nature is not possible for one who has envied the sparrow-hawk and the sea-eagle their 'powerful, tranquil movements', their energy, isolation and pride (p. 81).

Julien Sorel is thus shown, quite unsentimentally, to have been born either too late or too soon: too late to earn his generalship on the field of battle and become a Marshal of France at thirty-five, too soon to take competitive examinations and rise solely though his merits to the highest offices in the Republic: the destiny of Georges Pompidou, the peasant's grandson from the Auvergne who became President of France, was after all not so very different from what Julien Sorel's might have been under more favourable circumstances. We are all parvenus now, and Julien would have stood out in our midst far more triumphantly than in the Restoration drawing rooms of Paris or Verrières

His exemplarity is underscored by the parallels established by Stendhal with the story of Jesus, another carpenter's son whom society liquidated when he got above himself. 'It seems likely', Theodore Ziolkowski has commented on this curious circumstance, 'that Stendhal introduced the parallels for the double purpose of contrast and parody. Julien seizes every possible opportunity to re-enact the role of Jesus in order to unmask the fundamental lack of Christian sentiment in his own society. At the same time, the fact that Julien is so un-Christlike turns his role into a parody.' This kind of tension between seriousness and burlesque makes Stendhal the least complacent of the broadly humanistic novelists, and helps account for his fully deserved reputation. The moral dimension he introduces into his fiction is worlds away from the insufferable pieties of George Sand or Mrs Gaskell: it is more nervous—rather in the manner of Dickens and George Eliot—and a great deal less self-satisfied.

III

Stendhal's hesitancy over the true nature of Julien arises in part from the fact that he is aware of a marked streak of amorality in his hero, even of a potential criminality; like Dostoyevsky in the creation of Raskolnikov, Stendhal went to the criminal records for the source of his novel: Julien's story was inspired by that of Antoine Berthet, an ambitious blacksmith's son, executed some four years before the publication of *Scarlet and Black*, whose career bears a superficial resemblance to Julien's. But as so often is the case, this was yet another example of life imitating art; the misfortunes of the intelligent but penniless and humbly-born parvenu were merely exemplified by Berthet, they were not inaugurated by him. He suffered, as no doubt did many others whose cases lie buried in police files, from the *mal du siècle* which was already catching the imagination of writers. Stendhal's Julien was not the first parvenu of fiction, any more than Balzac's Eugène de Rastignac or Dickens's Pip or Mrs Craik's John Halifax were. The archetype probably goes back to the disrespectful mode of the picaresque, certainly to Marivaux's novel of 1734, *Le Paysan parvenu* ('The Upstart Peasant'), in which rogue-tales of the kind popularized in France by Lesage in his *Gil Blas de Santillane* during the early decades of the eighteenth century merge with the novel of manners to produce something closer to the parvenu stories of the nineteenth.

Adventures in *Le Paysan parvenu* still follow each other without much more to link them than chance ('le hasard' is an important concept in Marivaux); but there is the thread provided by the consistent central character, who is also the narrator, and by the upward progress of the *paysan parvenu* of the title. In its richness, its muddle, even its unfinishedness, Marivaux's book anticipates much to come in the novel, even though, or perhaps because, it is not so single-minded as *The Princess of Cleves* or *Dangerous Liaisons*. There are too many details to enable the work to be finished; like Sterne's *Tristram Shandy*, it would need to be very long at the pace set by the narrator if it were ever to be completed. The hero, Jacob, is wily; the novel he appears in has, like *Manon Lescaut* published three years earlier, a striking moral ambiguity. There are licentious passages and satires on spuriously devout ladies for whom the flesh is far from dead; for there pervades Marivaux's work generally a delicate eroticism. In this novel it takes the form of extended titillation about the relations between the social-climbing peasant Jacob and his employer Mademoiselle Habert, but everything is held back—there is no haste for consummation. That all is not as innocent as it appears, however, is shown in the passage which describes how Jacob, who has just married his employer and acquitted himself honourably on his energetic wedding night, finds himself attracted to other well-born mature women who proceed in rapid succession to succumb to his charms.

Although *Le Paysan parvenu* may not seem to take us much beyond the licentious trivia of the French eighteenth-century novel, it does foreshadow much that was to follow a hundred years later. In an essay on Henry James, collected in *The Liberal Imagination*, Lionel Trilling speaks of 'a great line of novels which runs through the nineteenth century as, one might say, the very backbone of its fiction.' These novels can be defined, he claims, by the character and circumstances of their heroes, and they include *Scarlet and Black*, *Old Goriot* and *Great Expectations*. 'The defining hero', he writes, 'may be known as the Young Man from the Provinces. He need not come from the provinces in literal fact, his social class may constitute his province. But a provincial birth and rearing suggest the simplicity and the high hopes he begins with—he starts with a great demand upon life and a great wonder about its complexity and promise. He may be of good family but he must be poor. He is intelligent, or at least aware, but not at all shrewd in worldly matters. He must have acquired a certain amount of education, should have learned something about life from books, although not the truth.'

It is not difficult to account historically for the emergence of this type. Nineteenth-century society was relatively stable, standing poised between two major revolutionary waves. The French and American revolutions, which were launched by and largely benefited the middle classes, had (except for dying convulsions in 1830 and 1848) run their course, and the major proletarian upheavals of the present century were not yet even foreshadowed: their harbinger, the event that so disturbed Flaubert, was the Paris Commune which did not occur until 1871. In such a transitional situation, in which most of the wealth was in the hands of a small newly-rich minority (a state of affairs exposed by a score of novels, from *Mary Barton* to *Hard Times*), the grip taken on the popular imagination by the archetype of the rising young man was understandable—at least as much as that, a little later, of the American Dream, which is the subject of Chapter 7, and which answered to a similar socio-economic concurrence of needs. In the embodying of such archetypes lesser novels are often more characteristic of the mode, because more limited by it, than great ones; for this reason I think it worthwhile to refer to a classic piece of Victorian sentimentality, a novel published by an ironic coincidence in the same year as *Madame Bovary:* Mrs Craik's *John Halifax, Gentleman.* The story turns—as does that of *Scarlet and Black, Great Expectations* and many others—on a cliché: but whereas Stendhal and Dickens transcend the cliché, Mrs Craik does not.

Nevertheless, her book is not negligible; it is certainly a lot livelier than Mrs Gaskell's ponderous first novel, *Mary Barton.* For all the sentimentality and girlish fantasy of the author's treatment of the love-affair between John Halifax and his wife (the novel was written some years before her marriage to G.L. Craik, one of the Macmillan partners), there is a ring of truth and a basic toughness, somewhat reminiscent of Charlotte Brontë, in the way she shows how Ursula is made into a better person then she would otherwise have been by her association with her husband John: 'he made me good', she says at the end, 'that was why I loved him'. But otherwise the emphatic moralism, the religiosity and the morbidity of the Victorian novel at its most characteristic dominate the book. It is bourgeois morality drama, a *comédie larmoyante* in which the virtues of sobriety, industry, thrift, chastity, and (reasonable) ambition are rewarded with conjugal bliss, family contentment, prosperity and an honoured name. It is almost aggressively middle-class: the aristocracy is looked upon as quite degenerate, and the narrator heaves an almost audible sigh of relief when John's favourite child 'narrowly escapes' becoming 'Viscountess Ravenel—future Countess of Luxmore', as if to marry into the nobility —an ambition nearly every mill-owner cherished for his daughters—were a fate worse than death: note the echoes of 'ravenous' and 'luxury' (in the sense of lust) in Mrs Craik's invention of aristocratic-sounding names. It is true she is liberal-minded about Catholic Emancipation and even prepared to make an effort to understand Jacobinism, but she shares her countrymen's ineradicable self-righteousness with regard to what she sees as the godless frivolity of the French, castigated with heavy authorial irony in this severe exchange between Lord Ravenel and Mrs Halifax:

'It was I who brought your son to Compiène—where he is a universal favourite, from his wit and liveliness. I know no one who is a more pleasant companion than Guy.'

Guy's mother bowed—but coldly.

'I think, Mrs Halifax, you are aware that the earl's tastes and mine differ widely—have always differed. But he is an old man, and I am his only son. He likes to see me sometimes, and I go—though, I must confess, I take little pleasure in the circle he has around him.'

'In which circle, as I understand, my son is constantly included?'

'Why not? It is a very brilliant circle. The whole court of Charles Dix can afford none more amusing. For the rest, what matters? One learns to take things as they seem, without peering below the surface. One wearies of impotent Quixotism against unconquerable evils.'

'That is not our creed at Beechwood,' said Mrs Halifax abruptly, as she ceased the conversation.

Chapter XXXV

It is not my intention, however, to poke fun at prejudice, no matter how widely shared or—as here crassly expressed, but to point up some interesting parallels with *Scarlet and Black* to whose subtle ironies, of course, Mrs Craik would have been quite deaf. But in her novel, as in Stendhal's, an orphan-type hero (John Halifax is of gentle birth but destitute) is taken up by a benefactor (here Abel Fletcher the Quaker) who, like the Marquis de la Mole, launches him in life almost as his own son; the young man later wins the heart of a lady raised in better circumstances than his own, who dies of grief eventually, shortly after his death. The lad largely educates himself, with some assistance from an understanding friend (in Halifax's case Phineas Fletcher, Abel's son, in Julien's, the old army surgeon who alone did not despise him as a weakling). In fact *John Halifax, Gentleman* reads like a bourgeois re-write of *Scarlet and Black:* the hero in both works cannot abide low-born acquaintances but aspires instinctively toward higher circles; in both books he is not mercenary, however, and will brook no slight to his pride; and both men excite envy by their success in life. But there the resemblance ends. Mrs Craik can be devastatingly arch: Stendhal never is; she exalts probity, decency and thrift: Stendhal is concerned with honour in the highest sense—truth to oneself—and with the very purpose and value of existence; with probity, in fact, in the existential rather than the social or material sense.

In so far as John Halifax can be said to exist outside the hagiography of Sunday-school manuals, his character does show a plausible development. But a great novelist like Stendhal has no difficulty in bringing his hero brilliantly to life, by showing him torn 'between the settled mediocrity of a secure and comfortable existence and all the. heroic dreams of youth' (p. 92). A rather similar 'quarrel with himself' exercises Pip in *Great Expectations*, but Dickens's conclusion, if less herioc than Stendhal's, who sends Julien to the block, is perhaps more in accord with ordinary decencies. Pip's life has effectively been poisoned by the meddling of his benefactor, the convict Magwitch, who like Ralph in James's *Portrait of a Lady* but with more plebeian coarseness, presumes to 'create' someone by means of cash: Ralph wants to make Isabel a lady and only succeeds in supplying her with the means of ensuring her unhappiness, and Magwitch wants to 'own' a gentleman (the revealing verb is his, of course, not mine). But these paymasters do achieve their purpose even if they would not immediately recognize the result: Isabel becomes a 'lady' in the fullest sense of that word by and through the sufferings she undergoes in becoming a lady in the more commonly received sense; and Pip is purified by his misfortunes to such an extent that he becomes a true 'gentleman', the sort that no money will buy.

Such a conclusion is remote from Stendhal's universe; and indeed its very remoteness points to one of the fundamental differences between the French and the English novel, in that for Dickens moral reintegration is the fruit the parvenu plucks at the end of his journey, whereas for Julien it is death. He covers himself not in glory but in blood, that is, his own 'scarlet'. As Jean-Jacques Mayoux puts it, 'Dickens writes the novel of success, reintegration, restitution, Stendhal the novel of failure and disaster'. The disaster in Stendhal's case, however, is something of a triumph, the apotheosis of a superman: 'nothing less than complete failure', writes Harry Levin in *The Gates of Horn*, 'will prove Julien's sincerity, vindicate his good faith, and demonstrate that he is no mere *arriviste*'; while Dickens's success is in a minor key (and certainly not the sort that Mrs Craik, whose hero moves from sleeping in the open air at the Quaker's tanyard to the comforts of Beechwood Hall, had in mind at all). Although both great novels are dramatic and expertly paced, *Great Expectations* is less perfect a work of art than *Scarlet and Black*—it relies heavily on coincidence of the most implausible kind, to mention only one simple weakness—but it is a greater moral achievement. *Scarlet and Black* may be a psychological *tour-de-force;* but *Great Expectations* offers an education and an enrichment of sensibility.

IV

My feeling that the parvenu theme—so intimately linked with the development of the novel, the parvenu genre—derives ultimately from the picaresque, is borne out by that magnificently cool study of a female *picaro*, Thackeray's *Vanity Fair*. Becky Sharp 'makes it', all right; and even though the 'hardened little reprobate' is severely punished for her sins in accordance with the prevailing morality, she survives and is even forgiven by her indulgent creator. If *John Halifax, Gentleman* is a pious version of the Julien Sorel story, *Vanity Fair* is a parodic one. Like Julien, Becky makes her way by her wits, though unlike Julien she is not too concerned over the ethical proprieties of her actions, and will take a snub provided it doesn't affect the cash-flow; and like him she is an arch-dissembler, a 'perfect performer' and a consummate hypocrite, oblivious of either religious feeling or family affection. But society gets the better of her in the end as it got the better of him: 'All her lies and her schemes', we are told, 'all her selfishness and her wiles, all her wit and genius had come to this bankruptcy'; in recognition of which, no doubt, Thackeray charitably leaves the question open as to how guilty she *really* was. Wicked she no doubt is, but hardly evil; it is right that he should not disdain claiming her as the heroine of his 'novel without a hero'. She certainly forces our admiration, as Thackeray obviously intends she should—he is responsible after all for setting up the most cloying and insipid foils for her to pit her wits against. Of course Becky stoops to actions (even to genteel prostitution, the narrator hints) which Julien would never have dreamt of: but to set the two characters side by side not only underlines Julien's parvenu nature but also the basic selfishness which, for all his finer qualities, he shares with Becky Sharp.

Another parodic study of the parvenu—and probably, with Theodore Dreiser's *An American Tragedy* and John Brain's *Room at the Top*, the last of the entire line—is *Felix Krull*, the novel Thomas Mann worked on at intervals throughout his creative life and published in an unfinished form just before his death in 1955. *Krull* parodies not only the picaresque (there is no doubt about the roguery of this hero), but also the more characteristically German *Bildungsroman*, or novel of education and of moral and spiritual development, in which Goethe's *Wilhelm Meister* is the prototype and Kafka's *America* a distant descendant. The classic *Bildungsroman* describes how an artistic temperament comes to terms with the demands of social life; so Mann's scapegrace hero—whose work of art is his life, and vice-versa—is also shown adjusting to the exigencies of existence, and rather more successfully than many others of the genre, for we leave him impersonating a marquis and seducing a magnificent Portugese beauty. When we recall that he starts out in life as a lift-boy, we are amazed at the parvenu's cheek and are prepared to be as indulgent to his actions—most of which are of dubious morality although he never becomes a complete scoundrel—as Thackeray is to Becky's (which were after all a good deal more wicked). Like Julien, in fact, Felix shows up and exploits the hollow conventions according to which society behaves and rewards behaviour. Krull feigns not to be able to answer the question whether his actions and those of others are 'artistic or fraudulent': and that essential ambiguity, which society, craving as it continually does to be amused, refuses to resolve, gives the clever parvenu his chance, and allows him to say, like Hamm in Beckett's play *Endgame,* 'Since that's the way we're playing it, let's play it that way'.

V

Stendhal is not an impeccable novelist, any more than Dickens or Tolstoy are. Camus once referred to 'curious examples of negligence' in his work: the kind of thing he probably had in mind was the inconsistency in Part I of *Scarlet and Black* between Chapter 5, where we are told that Julien's pupils slept in the same room as he did, and Chapter 9 where the plot requires that Julien occupy separate quarters. More substantial and serious, of course, is the way *The Charterhouse of Parma* was hastily and clumsily brought to an end in response to the publisher's strictures on its length. But considering that Stendhal was in the habit of writing the later chapters of a book as he corrected proofs of the earlier sections, the 'negligences' could have been a great deal worse. In any case probably the most important aspect ultimately of *Scarlet and Black,* for all its loose ends and occasionally inconclusive episodes, is its self-consciousness as a novel: the word '*roman*', indeed, crops up a couple of dozen times in the book. Had Julien and Madame de Rênal lived in Paris, where 'love is the child of novels', says Stendhal, fiction would have enlightened them about their position; for novels dictate conduct, and can corrupt. Of course Stendhal is talking ironically here as he so frequently does elsewhere; and in any case, French fiction, even *Dangerous Liaisons,* has always pretended that novels, in the bad sense of the term, were nothing to with itself. Stendhal tries to take his distance too: 'when Julien left Madame de Rênal's room a few hours later, it might be said, to adopt the language of novels', he writes, 'that he had nothing further left to wish for'. But it is clear Stendhal thinks well of his calling: of Julien he confides with mock deprecation, 'he will never make a good priest nor a good administrator. Natures yielding to emotion like this are good at most to make artists only'. The story of *Scarlet and Black* is in large measure the disillusionment of Julien the artist with the novel of his life: 'to tell the truth he was tired of heroism', and at the zenith of his achievement he claims 'my novel is at an end'.

For life is a novel, a novel is life; or is it? 'Why, my good sir', declares Stendhal is what has come to be taken as an attempt at an exact definition of realist fiction, 'a novel is a mirror journeying down the high road. Sometimes it reflects to your view the azure blue of heaven, sometimes the mire in the puddles on the road below. And the man who carries the mirror in his pack will be accused by you of being immoral! His mirror reflects the mire, and you blame the mirror! Blame the high road on which the puddle lies, and still more the inspector of roads and highways who lets the water stand there and the puddle form.' This passage is not about realism, however, it is about the morality of the fictional enterprise. Don't blame the teller, Stendhal is saying, blame the tale: the novelist's material is perfectly genuine. But we know—and I suspect Stendhal did too—that matters are not so simple; as Frank Kermode has written, 'novels have characters, even if the world has not': Julien, parvenu character in a parvenu genre, must die when his life-novel or novel-life comes to an end, when Madame de Rênal, reunited with him at the last, can declare with more meaning than she probably realizes: 'I'm really beginning to believe this strange novel!'

CHAPTER TWO

The
Refuge of Art

CHAPTER TWO

The Refuge of Art

*La littérature s'est mise à se sentir double: à la fois objet
et regard sur cet objet, parole et parole de cette parole,
littérature-objet et méta-littérature.*

ROLAND BARTHES

I

In the course of the nineteenth century, the novel established itself as a
genre of unparalleled variety, range and depth. The Romantic, Realist
and Naturalist movements deposited their alluvia on its shores and left
it with the contours which are now familiar and taken for granted. By
the beginning of our era, therefore, this sophisticated medium had no
more territory to conquer, and so turned in upon itself. The effect of that
development—which Malcolm Bradbury has gone so far as to call 'the
revolution in technique that Modernism accomplished in the novel'—are
still with us. The 'neo-moderns' (to use Frank Kermode's useful term)
have not, in our own day, progressed much beyond the achievements
of the 'paleo-moderns' in the early decades of this century, at least
as far as narrative technique is concerned.

The modernist phenomenon which I should like to call narrative
introversion or involution, and which Bradbury has described as 'an air
of the form's exhausting itself in each new work', needs to be carefully
distinguished from a somewhat analogous feature of earlier fiction,
'self-conscious narration'. This, as Wayne C. Booth has shown, was
fairly widespread in the seventeenth and eighteenth centuries, and
reached its culmination in *Tristram Shandy*. Although it inevitably
affected the form of fiction, its main effect was to draw attention to the
narrator who claimed—and frequently exercised—ostentatious tyranny
over his reader, anticipating and often cheating his expectations for comic
effect. Modernism, however, disdained what is after all a not very
subtle way of drawing attention to the irredeemably fictive nature of
fiction, and opted instead for forms which, by turning in upon

33

themselves, showed up the novel narrating itself. In other words, although the intention was not dissimilar, the earlier device drew attention to the autonomy of the narrator, the later technique to the autonomy of the fictive structure itself; and whereas the former was basically humorous, the latter's aim was serious and 'literary' in a way that would have been incomprehensible a century or so previously.

We have to go back to Henry James to see the origins of this development in modernist writing. James moved from a discreet awareness of the reader, in his earlier novels, to a deft connivance with the reader in his later books. In *The Ambassadors* of 1903, for instance, he lightly flits from one character to another in the dialogue, alternately illuminating for the reader the mystery which lies unspoken behind the spoken word:

> Strether could only listen and wonder and weigh his chance. 'And yet, affected as you are then to so many of your clients, you can scarcely be said to do it for love.' He waited a moment. 'How do we reward you?'
>
> She had her own hesitation, but 'You don't!', she finally exclaimed, setting him again in motion. They went on, but in a few minutes, though while still thinking over what she had said, he once more took out his watch; but mechanically, unconsciously, and as if made nervous by the mere exhilaration of what struck him as her strange and cynical wit. He looked at the hour without seeing it, and then, on something again said by his companion, had another pause. 'You're really in terror of him.'
>
> He smiled a smile that he almost felt to be sickly. 'Now you can see why I'm afraid of you.'

Part First, Chapter I

James, who calls himself Strether's 'chronicler', keeps in the background, but not out of sight, supplying us with precious information while hinting tantalizingly at what he does not care to mention. The connivance is overt in a remark like this: 'It came over him that Miss Gostrey looked perhaps like Mary Stuart; Lambert Strether had a candour of fancy which could rest for an instant gratified in such an antithesis'—James, it is clear, is equally gratified to draw our attention to the antithesis established between the idea of Maria Gostrey and Maria Stuart. This is the novel conscious of its reader indeed; and a further appropriate way of underlining it is the play on the forenames of Lewis Lambert Strether. 'It's the name of a novel of Balzac's!' exclaims Miss Gostrey delightedly, adding as a wry afterthought, 'but the novel's an awfully bad one'. These fictional characters are connoisseurs of fiction themselves.

In Joseph Conrad's novels the overt awareness of the complexity of fictional structures is carried even further. *Under Western Eyes* (1911) is narrated from two different points of view: that of an elderly British language-teacher, and that of a young Russian revolutionary, Razumov. The former introduces the story, but to supplement his obviously partial information he has recourse to Razumov's confessional diary. The teacher remains the principal narrator: he uses the diary to supplement his account. But he does not simply intercalate it; he edits it, building it into his own narration,which is thereby completed and diversified.

This is not simply a convenient device, as it might have been in less sophisticated narrative structures prior to the nineteenth century: it is the very essence of the novel. Since *Under Western Eyes* is a study in pre-revolutionary Russian dilemmas as seen by and for westerners, Conrad requires a narrator who will 'distance' the material and make it comprehensible to us, and the language-teacher effectively does this by acting as go-between. At the same time, the complexity, irrationality and mystery of the problem, from the western point of view, is rendered by the immediacy of the use of the diary.

In pursuit of this intention Conrad's virtuosity of narration is striking. The first part, after a disingenuous disclaimer that the narrator is no artist and so must be content to tell the story naively and straight, is based on Razumov's account of how he betrayed the conspirator Haldin to the Tsarist police, and ends on a question: where will the compromised Razumov take himself off to now? The second part takes the narrative abruptly back six months in time, to the Russian expatriate colony in Geneva into which the language-teacher has his *entrées*. This part leads us up to the arrival of Razumov in the colony, where he is accepted as a fugitive from the Tsar. We have the answer to the question we were left with at the end of the first part: he will infiltrate the Geneva colony as a police stooge. The narration can now revert to Razumov's viewpoint, which it does in the last parts, taking us forward in time to the gruesome rough justice by which Razumov pays for his ill-considered treachery. The different viewpoints converge: the end is with the narrator, the language-teacher who has watched the whole tragicomic episode unfold, not fully comprehending its import until Razumov's diary comes into his hands. Then only can he understand what happened, and take pen to paper and lay it before us, in all its Russian darkness and inscrutability. But, despite his denials, he is a competent storyteller, that is, a constructor of fictions. He does not tell it 'straight', as a newspaper account might; nor does he take us through the stages he himself went through as the 'Razumov mystery' gradually sorted itself out in his mind, as a sleuth might do. Rather, he shapes the material in a dramatic form, by straightaway conjuring up Razumov in Petersburg on the basis of the diary, the only possible source of information on that subject. In other words, like any other creator, he undertakes an imaginative reconstruction which is neither wholly true nor wholly false. He is, in fact, a novelist, or would be if Conrad were not the 'real' novelist.

This novel, indeed, appears coyly reluctant to be taken as a novel ('this is not a work of imagination', Penguin ed., p. 90); it feels unable to effect a smooth 'transition' between Petersburg and Geneva in space, and in time the shift from the execution of Haldin to a period situated six months earlier, while Haldin was still alive, with his mother and sister living at his instigation and suggestion in the security of exile. But under the smoke-screen of talk about not being capable of making a neat transition, the prose does just that. A similar artfulness can be observed in the following passage:

> The diary of Mr Razumov testifies to some irritation on his part. I may remark here that the diary proper consisting of the more or less daily entries seems to have been begun on that very evening after Mr Razumov had returned home.
> Mr Razumov, then, was irritated. His strung-up individuality had gone to pieces within him very suddenly.
> 'I must be very prudent with him,' he warned himself . . .
> p.78

Here the language-teacher introduces an interpretation of the feelings of Razumov which a direct transcription of the diary's contents could not achieve, since the diarist would hardly think of explaining his feelings in an intimate journal. By an impressive sleight-of-hand the teacher slips in the interpretation and makes it seem as if it had emerged unassisted from his source-material. The diary acts as he intends that it should, as a check on his own veracity, enabling him to carry conviction that his work is not a fiction. He is thus, once again, a very skilled novelist indeed. He provides an object-lesson in how to handle a difficult theme, manage transitions, and combine two different, though complementary, points of view.

But, once again, he is not the novelist: Conrad is. An eighteenth-century writer would have been only too happy to shield behind such an alias, and the majority of his readers would certainly have assumed that the teacher was the author. In its early days, the novel had a struggle to be taken seriously as an art-form; by Conrad's time this was of course no longer necessary. Conrad is thus not creating an alibi for himself. He signs the novel in his own name and later wrote a preface for it, as James was wont to do. He knows that his readers are sophisticated enough to take it for granted that the weaving of fictions is not a frivolous pursuit, but the arduous labour of an artist. So he can create, for their admiration, a creator creating a fiction before their eyes, and all the while convincing them of its basic verisimilitude.

The degree of self-conscious virtuosity shown by Conrad is fully characteristic of the modernist period, usually situated between 1890 and 1930. Perhaps its greatest exponent was Marcel Proust who, apart from early exercises and journeyman-pieces, wrote only one novel, the final volumes of which he never saw through the press: *Remembrance of Things Past* (1913-27). On one level, this is a realist novel of a life and a society, both of which grow old in the course of the narration. In the last volume, the narrator returns after many years' absence in sanatoria to the high Parisian circles of which he was once an assiduous member. In mingling with the guests at a large reception he is astonished to see how old his friends now appear, and it only gradually dawns upon him that this is because he, too, has grown old. Many of those he once knew are dead; a few are dying, and so are not at the reception; the rest he brings once again all on to the same stage, and ends his chronicle with them all about him.

But this is more than a realistic story; it is a poetic quest for the lost reality of the past. Man, says Proust, is a giant, standing on the living stilts of his years; it is possible for him, in rare and therefore precious moments of illumination, to span the intervening decades and relive, in all its perfect natural reality, a fragment of his past. For most of us the joy of these isolated instants is short-lived and soon forgotten. But for the artist they are an imperious command to preserve and hold the vision, jewel-like, in a setting of words. Thus, for Proust, literature is the most important thing there is: it alone can give retrospective pattern to a life. *Remembrance of Things Past* is therefore primarily the story of the birth of a literary vocation, and of the conception of the work we are engaged in reading. It is thus a supremely self-conscious novel within the modernist mode.

Confidence in literature as the remedy for time's depredations is not, however, easily won. Early in the closing volume Proust's narrator describes how, before falling asleep one night, he dips into the Goncourts' journal. His reading depresses him: he is envious of the brothers' powers of observation, and yet is simultaneously aware that their acute eye sees little that is worthwhile because, being quite uncritical, it misses the essential. Thus he is both gloomy because the Goncourts convince him of his own lack of literary 'gifts', and strangely relieved because literature, which he had esteemed so highly, seems capable only of elegant *belle-lettrism*, of no use to him in his desire to resurrect the past. There are two points to be made about this crucial passage.

In the first place, the eight pages he 'quotes' from the journal are not, of course, to be found there. Indulging in a favourite pastime of his, Proust is not excerpting, but pastiching; the material he lends the brothers is not theirs, but his own: he has them describe a dinner-party at the Verdurins' such as he himself described often enough in the early volumes of his novel, but in very different terms. Here we have the ultimate in literary self-awareness: one writer shown describing, in the manner of another, a situation of his own imagining, in order that he may appear to convince himself of his own inability to write.

Secondly, this is of course only a preamble to the triumphant demonstration a little later that the narrator can find both the incentive and the subject-matter which will enable him to become a writer after all. After his mystical experience in the Guermantes library, he foresees the time when (although he does not say so explicitly) the literary work he is contemplating writing will become the book we hold in our hands. The fictional wheel thus comes full circle, just as the two 'ways' of the earlier volumes (Swann's Way and the Guermantes Way) are seen in fact not to be as irreconcilable as in his youth he had always believed, and just as the George Sand novel, *François le champi,* which reminds him painfully of his mother's capitulation to his neurasthenic lack of will in the opening pages of the first volume, when fondled in the Guermantes library, is the instrument of the literary self-discovery which will redeem that very weakness. He then perceives that the 'essential book' he is contemplating writing is the 'only genuine book', which the writer does not have to invent, in the usual sense of the term, but to translate, because it exists potentially in each one of us. 'The duty and task of the writer', Proust concludes, 'are those of a translator'.

Nevertheless he insists, and rightly, that his book is not autobiography, but fiction, that is to say, art. Its construction, he says, will be elaborate, and he uses various metaphors, comparing it, for instance, to a cathedral, or a gown. Both, in their different ways, are elaborate structures, requiring time and patience, and the careful building of different materials into an overall scheme, the purpose of which only stands revealed when the whole is complete. Perhaps, like Musil's novel *The Man Without Qualities* (1930-43), it can never be completed because incompleteness is its real form; some cathedrals, after all, like the great chancel of Narbonne, stand unfinished 'as a consequence of the very scale of the architect's plan'.

Grand-scale fiction may well draw on autobiographical material, but only in the sense that the writer can only speak of what he has known, felt, or experienced. But by the same token, what he writes of will be more general in its import than was his own experience, for 'every reader is, when he reads, reading only about himself'. Proust's narrator thus has no regrets that his account of his love-affairs will, by veering towards the universal, commit infidelities towards the women he loved, for 'this profanation of my memories by unknown readers' who apply them to their own situation 'was carried out by 'myself beforehand' in the process of refracting them through the literary medium. Art, he says, defaces the names from the tombstones of the mind. In literary creation the individual experience is transformed into a 'spiritual equivalent': in discovering ourselves, we uncover the work of art that lies within us. It is by art alone that we can emerge from ourselves; a writer's style is not a simple matter of technique, he insists, but a vision. Proust's own style may seem tediously complicated to the hasty reader, but this is not so: he sought many ways of encompassing his thought, and moved forward by accretion, like an oyster making a pearl. For him, at least, it was all supremely worthwhile: 'the true life, life at last discovered and illuminated, the only life really lived', he asserts, 'is that of the writer'.

This high conception of the literary calling, together with a virtuosity which at this level of practice is but the subtlety of a complex art, are strongly active also in Proust's near-contemporary, James Joyce. He was truly the novelist of the 'form exhausting itself in each new work', becoming, as he advanced, ever more complex, at least in appearance. From *Portrait of the Artist,* which to some extent describes itself, he moved to *Ulysses,* that very modernist variation on the Odysseus theme, and *Finnegans Wake.* If there is unbroken thematic development, the formal progression is discrete: the fictionalized confession of the *Portrait* and the jocose epic poem of the *Wake* have little, structurally speaking, in common. They are both clearly modernist in manner, but it is *Ulysses* (1922) which is the modernist novel *par excellence.* The idea of reincarnating the wily Odysseus in a seedy advertisement canvasser, and of telescoping the hero's ten-year wanderings into twenty hours of a Dublin summer day, is characteristic of the ironic literary self-consciousness of Modernism. The trivial and everyday are thereby mythologized, and the contemporary individual attains to the stature of a legendary hero; but by the same token, the ancient epic is reborn in a new idiom, like a Bach concerto transcribed by Schoenberg. *Ulysses,* by reworking an old tradition, rejoins it; and that, as T.S. Eliot has shown us, is a valid way of respecting the past.

It is characteristic of Modernism that it should ponder the great literary archetypes of our civilisation: Thomas Mann's *Doktor Faustus* is another example of the same phenomenon. We know that Mann admired Joyce's aesthetic ambition, but he surpassed him in ironic intelligence. Mann was above all the shaping artist, moulding the destiny of his hero Castorp in *The Magic Mountain* (1924), or projecting himself ironically in his 'portrait of the artist as a confidence-trickster', *Felix Krull.* Although this subtle and witty work was written in old age it has its roots in the preoccupations of the early Mann and of the modernist novel generally.

For André Gide, too, the novel presented a challenge. He declined to call his early fictions 'novels', preferring the description 'tale' or 'farce' instead. It was not until 1926 that he published his only novel, *The Coiners,* in which a novelist named Edouard is writing a novel called *The Coiners;* concurrently, he keeps a diary from which quotations are liberally taken by Gide, who during the writing of his novel also kept a journal which he published soon after it. It is superficial to dismiss this as an artificial game with Chinese boxes: *The Coiners* is a sophisticated reflection on the nature of fiction, and is constructed in a complex but exceedingly neat and tidy fashion. The life it reflects however is muddled and cruel: murder, suicide, loveless defloration and adultery by proxy are its subject, although it also treats of consummated passion (albeit homosexual) and paternal devotion.

The fact that in the end the unhappiness, after some blood-letting, is resolved and a precarious order restored, is an ironic comment: literature is tidying up after life's bungling. Gide thus establishes an ironic distance between himself and both his hero Edouard and his own fictional construction through the very technique which critics have dismissed as baroque; it is significant that Edouard cites as his aesthetic ideal *The Art of the Fugue*, which another character dismisses as an abstract and boring monument. This novel, too, may seem abstract and boring, but in it Gide recognizes, as the writer's cardinal problem, the relationship between fiction and reality, since fiction is the artist's ever-renewed and ever-inadequate means of embracing the shifting and lively forms of reality. It is logical, then, that Gide should be as much interested in the history of a book's making as in the book itself. Counterfeit money plays a certain role in the plot, but it is obvious that false coin is here mainly intended as an ironic metaphor of the kind which lies behind Mann's *Confessions of Felix Krull* also.

Gide's novel is therefore a paradox, but not a sterile one: its aim is to disturb our complacency both about life and about fiction. It is close to the Flaubertian ideal of a 'novel without a subject' in the sense that it grows out of and through itself. And the description that Musil applied to *The Man Without Qualities* ('what the story that makes up this novel amounts to is that the story that was supposed to be told in it is not told') fits *The Coiners* equally well, and not only in that Edouard's novel is never finished and thus not imparted to us. Gide demonstrates, in other words, the autonomy of the fictional material, which gets out of hand and commits violence before being brought to heel and restrained within some semblance of order. If life were not sanguinary disorder, it is implied, the story that is not told could always be told.

It is no accident that the 'portrait of the artist' theme is the modernist novel's most persistent motif. It runs through Conrad's teacher of languages, through Proust's Marcel finding his vocation in the library of a city mansion, to Mann's Tonio Kröger, Joyce's Stephen Dedalus and Gide's Edouard. This need cause no surprise: if narrative form is involuted in this period, it is natural for the novelist to look hard at himself also, and scrutinise his own features as his art scrutinises itself.

An art form preoccupied with its aesthetics is the kind of rare flower that only a fully mature plant can produce. There is the attendant danger of decadence through in-breeding; perhaps the great novels of early Modernism were saved from this because they were, in

Frank Kermode's words, 'all characterised by a kind of formal desperation'. It is this 'desperation' which ensures that structural involution in this period transcends narcissistic self-satisfaction and attains to the lucidly critical self-awareness of an art of a uniquely fertile and original kind.

II

Just as it is characteristic of Modernism that it should ponder the great literary archetypes of our civilisation, so post-Modernism, too, looks back to the past. But it does so in a looser, freer way. *Ulysses* reworks the Odyssey, but Beckett's *Molloy*—as we shall see in Chapter 5—merely reflects it: the allusions are more subterranean, even incidental. Works written since World War II, like *Molloy*, tend to show an awareness of the classics which is much more oblique than Joyce's or Thomas Mann's; and yet the presence is there, and often strongly felt.

This is the case, for instance, with Iris Murdoch's novel *A Severed Head* (1961). In it a group of characters rearrange their relationships at least once and in some cases twice during the course of the action. Specifically, the hero Martin Lynch-Gibbon realizes he loves neither his wife Antonia not his mistress Georgie, but Honor Klein, the sister of his wife's lover. Palmer Anderson, the brother in question, starts the novel as the lover both of Honor his half-sister and of Antonia Lynch-Gibbon, and ends it leaving for New York in the company of Martin's ex-mistress Georgie Hands. Antonia herself, having run away from Palmer whose attitude towards her changes dramatically once Martin has discovered him and Honor in bed together, goes back briefly to Martin before declaring that her true passion is Alexander, Martin's brother, who has been her lover on and off for many years. But before he leaves for Rome with her, Alexander has had time to become engaged to Georgie Hands and provoke her to attempt suicide. The only character not linked sexually to any other (although it is implied she has her own affairs elsewhere) is Rosemary, the *divorcée* sister of Martin and Alexander. And the only two characters who have nothing sexually to do with each other are Alexander and Honor Klein. Otherwise, Antonia loves Martin, Palmer and Alexander, Georgie loves Martin, Alexander and Palmer, and Honor is loved by Palmer and Martin: all in that order. I put Honor's attachments in the passive voice because she is the rather mysterious dynamo who generates the tensions which cause the others to act; she herself takes no initiatives, except perhaps at the very end when having seen the others off the stage she calls on Martin with the evident intention of offering herself to him.

This plot, inevitably rather crude-sounding in summary, is by no means as frivolous as might appear at first sight. In the final pairings each hitherto morally blind partner (Martin, Antonia and Georgie) is linked up with a lucid one (respectively Honor, Alexander and Palmer), undoubtedly for his or her good. It is undeniably better for Martin to grow up into full moral adulthood: he has tended in the past to take refuge in filial relationships with women. The shock of Antonia's adulteries, and of Georgie's misadventures culminating in her departure in Palmer's company, and above all of his own demonic passion for the 'severed head', Honor, hurls him brutally but salutarily from his cosy Eden. As for Antonia, she has to stop enjoying the possession of three men, who flatter different facets of her make-up, and settle for one of them. And Georgie, abandoned by one brother after the other, learns the hard way that a girl makes herself a doormat at her peril. Under the surface comedy of this game of musical beds lies a closely-argued moral statement: that to play with people is to hurt them, that to abase oneself in love is to invite humiliation, and that only upon mutual respect can a mature and adult love be based. Under the dazzling appearance of comic contingency, in other words, lies the tougher substance of an almost tragic determinism.

The subterranean parallel with Racine—of the kind I alluded to earlier—is striking. Like Racine, Iris Murdoch achieves what one critic has described as 'the paradox of combining uncertainty and predetermination'. Just as, in spite of the numerous peripeteias in *Andromaque* (in which A loves B, who loves C, and so on), Pyrrhus unwittingly moves closer to his rendezvous with death, so Martin Lynch-Gibbon moves closer to *his* rendezvous with a too-long-deferred and therefore deeply painful and unsettling realization of his emotional immaturity. The moment in which he grasps the fact that he is 'desperately, irrevocably, agonizingly in love with Honor Klein' is akin to the moment when a Racinian hero or heroine realizes that he or she is trapped and cannot escape the tragic net closing in around. But, as in *Andromaque* and other major tragedies by Racine, the 'serried determinism of the action only becomes apparent at the *dénouement*'. Like Oreste, who cries out against his own helplessness in the face of his destiny, Martin perceives that he 'was chosen, and relentlessly, not choosing'. The suspense in *Andromaque*, the rabbit-out-of-hat surprises in *A Severed Head*, exist merely to distract the reader temporarily from the inexorable workings of fate and the outcome of what Martin calls his 'monstrous love, a love out of such depths of self as monsters live in'—the love of a Hermione or of a Phèdre. 'You cannot cheat the dark gods', Honor tells Martin at one point: the same hard lesson has to be learned by Racine's protagonists also. It is true that they usually die for it whereas Iris Murdoch's people on the whole do not. But the difference is merely one of convention: the process is essentially the same.

III

'It is sometimes only at the precise moment when we think that everything is lost' (Proust writes in *Time Regained*) 'that the intimation arrives which may save us': Marcel's anxiety on the subject of his death had ceased, he tells us, at the moment when he had unconsciously recognized the taste of the little *madeleine*, for he made the discovery of the 'destructive action of Time' at the very instant when he conceived 'the ambition to make visible, to intellectualize in a work of art, realities that were outside Time'. One of the most characteristic motifs of the modernist novel concerns the ways the narrator—who is usually also the chief protagonist—seeks his salvation through the art of fiction, and as often as not through the very novel the reader holds in his hands. If the sophistication of the mode is typical of Modernism, its origins lie further back in the nineteenth-century epics of failure, of which Flaubert's *Sentimental Education* is the great archetype. But Flaubert's story of Frédéric Moreau's mediocrity—which preserves him from total disaster à la Julien Sorel as it denies him the fulfilment of his extravagant dreams—was foreshadowed by a less well-known and indeed less brilliant novel, but a book which, nevertheless, incarnates the type to something approaching perfection: *Dominique*, the semi-autobiographical novel which the painter Eugène Fromentin published in 1863. It could almost be Stendhal written in a minor key: not 'do or die' but 'fail and live on'.

The limpidity of *Dominique* is in the best French tradition; as a story told to a third party it reminds us formally of *Manon Lescaut*, and the childhood sections look forward to *Le Grand Meaulnes*. It cost Fromentin much effort (he said his 'wicked book' caused him 'great disgust'), as Flaubert's *Madame Bovary* did him, and at one point there is a sentence the rhythms of which could almost have been Flaubert's doing. Was Fromentin influenced by Flaubert, or was the sentence just coincidence?

> And with my face hidden in my hands, I remained there, looking into the void, seeing before me my whole life, immense, dubious and as unfathomable as a precipice.

Like *Scarlet and Black* this 'trop peu romanesque' fiction is a self-conscious novel: Dominique is trying to be a writer, but 'I came across my own story', he admits, 'in the works of others, some of which are immortal'. Perhaps one of them was *La Nouvelle Héloïse*, which tells how another virtuous wife tries to cure a young man of an adulterous love. Rousseau's Julie has been metamorphosed into Fromentin's Madeleine, and Saint-Preux into his Dominique; and as a result the novel has become recognizably more middle-class over the hundred-year interval, even to the extent of being proud of its 'dénouement bourgeois'. But the theme remains the same: later on, André Gide was to orchestrate the pathos of unconsummated love and sexual failure in *Strait is the Gate*, a novel which, while surpassing it, owes much to *Dominique*; indeed a passage near the end which Fromentin was going to insert, and then thought better of, contains the germ of Gide's development of the idea. And a few years later, of course, Flaubert was himself to develop the theme of 'sentimental education' which underlies *Dominique*; Madeleine's confession of love for the hero is not unlike Madame Arnoux's for Frédéric.

A novel as clearly central to the French tradition as *Dominique* might be expected to be one of the greatest of that line. It is not. It is too diaphanous; it falls well short of being a masterpiece; indeed it does so with its eyes open: it is about mediocrity, and that includes literary mediocrity. Dominique knows that posterity will judge his literary work harshly, as harshly as he does that of the majority of his contemporaries; and Fromentin is certainly speaking through his hero on this subject as on others. Dominique, enthralled, watches a great tenor singing beautifully what he does not feel, and yet knows full well that he himself does not possess the sort of talent which would allow him to express even what he does feel; so he burns his manuscripts in despair. In other words, this is a fine novel about the impossibility of writing a great one: Dominique is presented throughout as a man whose greatest achievement has been to recognize his own limitations.

The fact that Fromentin was a professional painter shows in the visual precision of his fictional technique: gloomy weather dominates in sad moments, and good weather in happy ones. The whole reminds one to some extent of Ingres (although Fromentin, wishing to keep his distance from his *alter ego* Dominique, makes him ignorant of painting); there is a certain glacé quality about the writing which recalls Ingres' pictorial style. And the accent on *ennui*, world-weariness, is characteristic of an age when Baudelaire and Flaubert were active. *Dominique* is thus very much of its time, and as Dominique himself shrewdly realized, books written like that could only hope to afford 'their contemporaries a passing diversion'. But the impotent cry uttered by Dominique, 'I have no will; I am governed by fate' makes him of interest to us as being in his own modest, *bürgerlich* way a kind of hero, as typical of his stolid age as Julien Sorel was of his more wicked one.

From *Dominique* it may seem a far cry to *A la recherche du temps perdu* by Marcel Proust; but both novels deal in different ways with the theme of artistic failure. Fromentin worked out a sense of his own inferiority as a painter in a fiction about a failed novelist; and Proust overcame numerous socio-sexual conflicts in a novel which drew upon, but at the same time transcended and mythified, his own autobiography. And in the last volume of his masterpiece he probed carefully into the nightmare which haunts every creator: that he will not succeed in expressing what he feels impelled to express. This Proust did through metaphor. The closing pages take on a special poignancy from the fact that the narrator feels death a pressing threat to the work which must be written if his life is to be saved: 'like the seed, I should be able', he says, 'to die once the plant had developed, and I began to perceive that I had lived for the sake of the plant without knowing it'.

Another great work of fiction of the modernist period which—albeit more ambivalently and ironically—treats the work of art as a kind of ecstatic orgasm projecting the soul of the artist into immortality is Thomas Mann's *Death in Venice*. Aschenbach, entirely conquered by his young idol, feels one day a sudden urge to write; and the occasion is not lacking:

> News had reached him on his travels that a certain problem had been raised, the intellectual world challenged for its opinion on a great and burning question of art and taste. By nature and experience the theme was his own: and he could not resist the temptation to set it off in the glistering foil of his words. He would

write, and moreover he would write in Tadzio's presence. This lad should be in a sense of his model, his style should follow the lines of this figure that seemed to him divine; he would snatch up this beauty into the realms of the mind, as once the eagle bore the Trojan shepherd aloft. Never had the pride of the word been so sweet to him, never had he known so well that Eros is in the word, as in those perilous and precious hours when he sat at his rude table, within the shade of his awning, his idol full in his view and the music of his voice in his ears, and fashioned his little essay after the model Tadzio's beauty set: that page and a half of choicest prose, so chaste, so lofty, so poignant with feeling, which would shortly be the wonder and admiration of the multitude.

Penguin ed., pp. 52-53

It is just as well for the world, Mann continues drily, that it usually knows very little about the origins of the works it admires or the conditions from which they spring. This exquisite *opus posthumus* of Aschenbach's 'strangely unnerves' its creator: 'when he put aside his work and left the beach', the narrator tells us, 'he felt exhausted, he felt broken—conscience reproached him, as it were after a debauch '

But elsewhere in the story Mann makes it clear that he thinks Aschenbach is an artist of a very high order: not quite of the very highest, since he has allowed one side of his nature (the orgiastic, Dionysian element) to become atrophied through neglect, but a considerable writer nevertheless. When the stately grace of his highly-polished prose is informed by the passion of Eros, as is the case with this last perfect fragment, it can be expected that it will be truly and not ironically presented as a masterpiece. If it is not so described by Mann this is because he wished to have his cake and eat it: to offer a stern moral critique of Aschenbach and his ilk while at the same time upholding the ideals of Greek 'plasticity' which the venerated author represents. As T.J. Reed concludes, *Death in Venice* remains ambiguous, 'not just in the sense that its many levels of meaning constitute complexity, but also in that there is a degree of uncertainty in the final impression it leaves' (introduction to the 'Clarendon German Series' edition).

Equally oblique is the hope of regeneration through art which is seen in Alain-Fournier's classic *Le Grand Meaulnes* (usually known in this country under the title *The Lost Domain*), a novel which appeared interestingly enough in 1913, the same year as *Swann's Way* by Proust.

The story is familiar to all readers of fiction: a boy meets a beautiful girl in a mysterious, exotic chateau, and when he becomes a man, marries her and loses her shortly afterwards through her death in childbirth. It is something of a deliberate exercise in nostalgia, Watteau-esque, a desperate attempt to recapture childhood sensations. As such it appeals to all grown-up schoolboys and schoolgirls: the atmosphere is that of pre-adolescent play, with dens and expeditions in the spirit of *Robinson Crusoe*, which is frequently evoked. A letter of Alain-Fournier's makes this clear:

> The hero of my book, Meaulnes, is a man whose childhood was too beautiful. He carries it about with him like a burden throughout his adolescence. At rare moments it seems that the entire imaginary paradise of his childhood world will come to life at the end of his adventures, or leap up at one of his gestures.
>
> Letter to Jacques Rivière, 4 April 1910

The novel therefore firmly rejects adult experience. Girls are truly pure, men are clean-limbed and noble of heart. There is a refusal of loss of innocence implied in the recoil from sexuality when Meaulnes, in answer to a signal—a prearranged boyish call for help from his brother-in-law—leaves his bride (pregnant, incredibly) on the very first day of their honeymoon. Life has been handed on, in Meaulnes's unborn child, with only a minimal loss of chastity. There is, as we might expect, more than a hint of misogyny about all this: women are declared to be incapable of appreciating men's problems, and one suspects an element of homosexuality in the narrator François's affection for Meaulnes: we are told, for instance, of 'a friendship more charged with pathos than a great love-affair'. A rather 'fevered' atmosphere thus surrounds the book: there is in it a breathless air of hyper-reality and excitement which is reminiscent of Gérard de Nerval's classic tale *Sylvie*. But unlike *Sylvie*, Alain-Fournier's novel is totally lacking in either humour or irony. If it has been so successful it is for non-literary reasons; apart from the artful exploitation of mystery and suspense, and the recurrent image of the labyrinth (happiness is always portrayed as being at the end of a maze), the novel is devoid of aesthetic interest. Its appeal is ascribable to nostalgia and to resentment at (or apprehension about) having to grow up, a feeling Jean Anouilh has pandered to in the theatre. As a work of art *Le Grand Meaulnes* is psychologically too simple-minded to sustain serious

criticism, and in spite of a neat construction which ties up all the ends
there are lapses of style which mar its much-vaunted formal
perfection. Like *The Laurels are Cut Down* it remains a curious novel
and a literary case, offering a modernist variant on the theme of courtly
love, and a fairy-tale for reluctant adults. But even as an exploration of
the world of childhood, it does not begin to compare with *Swann's
Way*.

Nevertheless whatever happens to Meaulnes and his abandoned
bride, the narrator François not only manipulates the story—where
necessary dislocating the time-sequence to conceal his own emotional
involvement in it—but also exploits it, not unlike Proust's Marcel, to
bring about his own birth into art: throughout Meaulnes's whole
bizarre adventure François's concern is to write, and his first essay as
an author—undoubtedly a liberating one for him, whatever we may
think of it—is the novel we are given to read.

Narrators still continue today the modernist tradition of depicting
and exploring their own salvation through art, deriving, as Martin
Sorrell has put it, consolation for the disappointments of life 'through
an artistic re-creation of that which has been meaningful'. This is
especially true of Claude Simon's greatest work, *Histoire,* which was
first published in 1967. This novel is, as it were, 'expelled' into the
realm of art somewhat as the 'gelatinous tadpole' (which is the narrator
in the first weeks of his being) will be born into an existence which will
inexorably include the writing of the narrative we are asked to read.
The pain of existence, the anguish of literary creation are twin aspects
of the struggle for being against nothingness, which forms the warp of
Histoire, and the precariousness of the enterprise is admirably
summed up in the novel's closing paragraph. In it, the narrator
imagines his mother, recently pregnant with him, leaning over a
counter to write one of the hundreds of postcards which he will later
come across in middle age when clearing out a piece of family furniture
he is forced to sell to pay his debts. Unpleasant as his situation is, not
only financially but (since his marriage has broken up) emotionally
also, discovering the postcards in this accidental manner permits a
kind of salvation: he will compose the text which we read on the basis
of these ephemeral, poignant family documents. The very last
paragraph of the novel thus concludes this exercise in fictive
reconstruction, at the same time as it recalls the launching of the
narrator himself into existence:

taking refuge in the shop of some kind of merchant probably the one who had sold her the postcard a Mr S.S. Ohashi with yellow skin watching her writing on a corner of a table or the counter the lady bending over, her mysterious bust of white flesh swathed in lace that bosom which already perhaps was bearing me in its shadowy tabernacle a kind of gelatinous tadpole coiled around itself with its two enormous eyes its silkworm head its toothless mouth its cartilaginous insect's forehead, me? . . .

translated by Richard Howard

We have come a long way, in *Histoire*, with its modest tones of disillusionment, from the defeated aspirations recorded in *Dominique* and *Sentimental Education*, and even from the difficult birth into art celebrated in *Time Regained* and *Death in Venice*, but men still cling to the noble belief that the act of creating fictions will redeem their otherwise irredeemable condition. We cannot help aspiring to the sole permanence available to us. Humbert Humbert, at the end of *Lolita*, calls it 'the refuge of art': for it represents, he realizes, the only immortality which he and his beloved Dolores Haze can ever hope to share.

CHAPTER THREE

Persuasive Rhetorics
and the
Rhetoric of Persuasion

Persuasive Rhetorics
and the Rhetoric of Persuasion

> *Now in prison, in freedom, he went over his*
> *actions again in his mind, and he did not find*
> *them so stupid or so absurd as they had seemed to*
> *him at the fatal time in the past. 'Why does my*
> *action strike me as so hideous?' he kept saying to*
> *himself. 'Is it because it was a crime? What does*
> *"crime" mean? My conscience is clear'*

DOSTOYEVSKY

I

Albert Camus's appeal, as a novelist, is largely to the emotions, not to the intellect — he is a stirring but not particularly profound writer. He was killed in a road accident in 1960, by which date it was fairly clear that his major works had been written, and that he might have been led either to take refuge in the kind of obscure ironics which inform *The Fall*, or to caricature himself in the role of professional humanist which seems to have been forced upon him by the award of the Nobel Prize.

His first and indeed his only great novel, *The Outsider*, was completed by 1940, but it did not appear for two years after that because of the difficulties of book production in war conditions. The first words of the book, 'Mother died today. Or, maybe, yesterday; I can't be sure', established its unique tone, and revealed that Camus had learned the lessons not only of Hemingway but also of Kafka. Here is the opening section, in Stuart Gilbert's translation:

> Mother died today. Or, maybe, yesterday; I can't be sure. The telegram from the Home says: *Your mother passed away. Funeral tomorrow. Deep sympathy.* Which leaves the matter doubtful; it could have been yesterday.
>
> The Home for Aged Persons is at Marengo, some fifty miles from

53

Algiers. With the two-o'clock bus I should get there well before
nightfall. Then I can spend the night there, keeping the usual vigil
béside the body, and be back here by tomorrow evening. I have fixed
up with my employer for two days' leave; obviously, under the
circumstances, he couldn't refuse. Still, I had an idea he looked
annoyed, and I said, without thinking: 'Sorry, sir, but it's not my
fault, you know.'

Afterwards it struck me I needn't have said that. I had no reason
to excuse myself; it was up to him to express his sympathy and so
forth. Probably he will do so the day after tomorrow, when he sees
me in black. For the present, it's almost as if Mother weren't really
dead. The funeral will bring it home to one, put an official seal on
it, so to speak . . .

I took the two-o'clock bus. It was a blazing hot afternoon. I'd
lunched, as usual, at Céleste's restaurant. Everyone was most kind,
and Céleste said to me, 'There's no one like a mother'. When I left
they came with me to the door. It was something of a rush, getting
away, as at the last moment I had to call in at Emmanuel's place to
borrow his black tie and mourning-band. He lost his uncle a few
months ago.

I had to run to catch the bus. I suppose it was my hurrying like
that, what with the glare off the road and from the sky, the reek of
petrol and the jolts, that made me feel drowsy. Anyhow, I slept most
of the way.

Penguin ed., pp. 13-14

Beside this vague groping by the hero for some meaning in a chaotic
world, Antoine Roquentin, the hero of Sartre's novel *Nausea*, seems a
pillar of rationality and good sense. Meursault, on the contrary, is a man
of the senses, alive basically only to the feel of the sun and the sea on his
body. Abstract conceptions like 'grief and remorse' are mere words to
him, without any tangible connotation. Roquentin remains what has
been called a 'philologist': one for whom words, and especially written
words, have the power to order and sort out the problems and
difficulties of everyday life. Like Sartre himself, whose autobiography
is entitled, revealingly, *Words*, Roquentin can attempt to come to grips
with his metaphysical anguish through the medium of language. In
short, he is an intellectual, like his creator, a writer, a reader. He reads
the words of others and writes his own words on the basis of them—he
is an intermediary, a no doubt humble one, but an intermediary none

the less in the chain of human intellectual development.

Not so Meursault. He doesn't read anything to speak of, and hardly writes a line. He just feels. Of course we have to accept that somehow his confession was written down, but Camus does not concern himself with this question—rightly perhaps, because he at least avoids Sartre's clumsiness in beginning *Nausea* as if it were an actual diary. But there are two difficulties about the book; whether these are more apparent than real is the issue this chapter is concerned with. First of all Camus himself is an intellectual, a 'philologist', and there may be something artificial in an intellectual portraying a non-intellectual; sooner or later the author's sophistication and subtleties will show through in the character. This seems to happen in *The Outsider*: the admirably neutral opening, derived as I have said from Kafka and Hemingway and which has led to much fertile French writing in more recent years, appears to become 'clever' when, after the murder of the Arab, Meursault starts to reflect on the 'big' issues of life. The passage where he shakes the priest who has come to try and bring him to thoughts of religion before execution, is of course superb—especially the cry 'none of his certainties was worth one strand of a woman's hair'—so superb that we are in some danger of forgetting that this sublime rhetoric is uttered by a man who up to this point has been presented to us as an inarticulate sun-worshipper:

> I don't know how it was, but something seemed to break inside me, and I started yelling at the top of my voice. I hurled insults at him, I told him not to waste his rotten prayers on me; it was better to burn than to disappear. I'd taken him by the neckband of his cassock, and, in a sort of ecstasy of joy and rage, I poured out on him all the thoughts that had been simmering in my brain. He seemed so cocksure, you see. And yet none of his certainties was worth one strand of a woman's hair. Living as he did, like a corpse, he couldn't even be sure of being alive.

> p. 118

Is it still Meursault speaking here, the reader wonders, or Camus the intellectual, steeped in his Dostoyevsky and his Kierkegaard, talking at us over Meursault's head? After all, the plot of the first version of *The Outsider* closely resembled *Crime and Punishment,* and in both works exceptionality is held to be closely allied with criminality. Dostoyevsky does of course show Raskolnikov's error in believing both that sin can lead to immense benefits for mankind, and that his only crime was to have failed in the attempt: but this enlightenment comes only at the very end in the novel's Siberian epilogue, in which he accepts his punishment as an act of atonement.

The second difficulty about *The Outsider* is a formal one connected with the first. The book, like Hemingway's *A Farewell to Arms,* opens brilliantly, but the promise of the beginning appears unfulfilled in both cases. Hemingway degenerates rapidly into an embarrasing 'tough-guy' manner, the Rock Hudson syndrome. As for Camus, he seems to slip into grandiloquence about Life and Death which is so dear to the French intellectual. Notwithstanding its deceptive brevity and limpid aspect, the novel seems, according to this view, to raise a number of critical questions. In his classic study of these issues, *The Rhetoric of Fiction,* Wayne C. Booth declares that he finds the end especially baffling: 'why', he wonders, should Meursault 'on the brink of freedom' desire 'howls of execration' rather than expressions of 'benign indifference', and how, he asks, can Meursault's final affirmation ('I was happy') relate to what Booth considers 'the many negations of the work'? No wonder he decides that Meursault is 'confused.' And Cyril Connolly, in his introduction to the first English edition, confessed himself pained by the 'failure of sensibility on the part of Camus that the other sufferer in his story, the Moorish girl whose lover beats her up and whose brother is killed when trying to avenge her, is totally forgotten'. Other critics, again, while admitting to the spell which Meursault's story casts, declare themselves puzzled about the point in time at which it claims to be written: in some passages they feel it reads like a diary set down in the heat of the event, at other moments it resembles normal prose narrative, except in so far as it is told in the ambiguous *passé composé* or perfect tense, which in French can indifferently refer to a very recent past (corresponding to the English 'I have done'), or to a more distant epoch (as in the English 'I did'). Faced with the question 'is Meursault writing a diary, or isn't he?', to which there appears no immediately satisfying answer, the reader may be forgiven for concluding that Camus was simply being inconsistent. But is this very likely? Some works, like Arthur Adamov's *Professor Taranne,* give so distinct an impression of sustained inspiration that we are not surprised when the author informs us that he did in fact write quickly and without hesitation. There is not much doubt that *The Outsider* comes into this category: there are only minor variants between the first manuscript draft and the published text. It is clear that whatever we may think of the artistic success or failure of the book, Camus, at least, was satisfied with what he was doing and chose his tenses with deliberate care.

Up till now, too, critics have tended to assume that attitudes expressed in *The Myth of Sisyphus* and other writings are directly transposed in imaginative form in *The Outsider*, without making sufficient allowance for differences created, even imposed, by the change of genre. For me the answer is that Camus may well have intended to write a novel in order to exploit a variant form for the exposition of ideas set out elsewhere but, in the act of writing, the fiction itself—with its own life and its own dynamic—took over and outstripped the rather simplistic romantic philosophy he expounds elsewhere. As a result he embodied in *The Outsider* a theme which his reading of three favourite authors—Stendhal, Dostoyevsky and Kafka—made him conversant with and eager to handle in his own way, by transposing it into the North African context with which he was familiar. This theme—of the embattled outcast persecuted both by society and by the malevolent fates which govern human destiny—is adumbrated in another work which otherwise bears little relation to *The Outsider*: Conrad's ironic tragedy *Lord Jim*.

II

The story of *Lord Jim* is well known. An upright young merchant seaman—a clean-limbed parson's son, very much 'one of us' as Conrad's narrator Captain Marlow puts it—is disgraced because he and the other officers in command of a pilgrim ship abandon it when they believe (mistakenly, as it turns out) that it is in imminent danger of foundering. Thereafter Jim makes a living as a ship-chandler's water-clerk in various Eastern ports, staying in each only so long as his incognito holds good. As soon as it is penetrated 'he retreats in good order towards the rising sun'. At last, 'when his keen perception of the Intolerable drove him away for good from seaports and white men, even into the virgin forest, the Malays of the jungle village, where he had elected to conceal his deplorable faculty, added a word to the monosyllable of his incognito. They called him Tuan Jim: as one might say—Lord Jim'. But his tragedy is merely suspended, it is not played out. An Iago-figure by the name of Cornelius brings about his final downfall. This time, however, Jim doesn't funk: he goes out to meet his destiny, and dies with 'a proud and unflinching glance' in his eyes.

The faithful Marlow keeps alive his memory and justifies him to a hostile and unforgiving world; but not (and this is a significant point in connection with *The Outsider*) before his own resisting scepticism has been overcome, and he has himself become convinced of Jim's essential innocence. This conversion takes place not because of what Marlow learns at the official inquiry into the incident—which results in the cancellation of Jim's certificate and the abrupt termination of his career as a mariner—but at the end of a long evening during which he receives the young man's confidences and is mesmerized into viewing matters from another point of view. As Novalis put it in Conrad's aptly-chosen epigraph, 'It is certain any conviction gains infinitely the moment another soul will believe in it'.

But before this happens it is quite clear that Marlow considers Jim to be very culpable. 'I thought to myself', he muses, 'if this sort can go wrong like that . . . I waited to see him overwhelmed, confounded, pierced through and through, squirming like an impaled beetle . . . I wanted to see him squirm for the honour of the craft'; so much so that until 'I became positive in my mind that the inquiry was a severe punishment to that Jim,' and 'his facing it—practically of his own free will—was a redeeming feature in his abominable case', Marlow is not at all sympathetic. He makes contact with the miscreant under circumstances which, characteristically of everything connected with Jim, are not without a macabre grotesqueness (Jim spins round and challenges him for an imaginary insult); he invites Jim to dinner, as much to placate him as anything. Soon the very guileless simplicity of the disgraced young mate is 'appealing at sight to all my sympathies' in spite of Marlow's perfect awareness that 'no man ever understands quite his own artful dodges to escape from the grim shadow of self-knowledge'. With all the directness of the undevious and the uncomplicated, Jim asks Marlow what he would have done in similar circumstances. This *ad hominem* approach takes the older man by surprise: 'before I could recover,' he says, 'he went on . . . "I don't want to excuse myself . . . but I would like somebody to understand—somebody—one person at least" '. And the man upon whom, Ancient Mariner-like, he has battened in order to justify himself in his anguished search for absolution, admits freely that he is 'swayed . . . as if the obscure truth involved were momentous enough to affect mankind's conception of itself', and takes his part before the silent, invisible audience listening to Marlow's tale. 'Frankly', says the veteran officer—whose outstanding quality is frankness—'frankly, had I been there, I would not have given as much as a counterfeit farthing for the ship's chance to keep above water to the end of each successive second . . . It's extraodinary how he could cast upon you the spirit of his illusion. I listened as if to a tale of black magic at work upon a corpse.' Before the evening was over (Marlow tells us, only half in jest) 'I was moved to make a solemn declaration of my readiness to believe implicitly anything he thought fit to tell me'.

The rhetoric which the overpoweringly simple Jim employs with largely unconscious skill to convince the experienced and sceptical older sailor is based upon a 'strange illusion of passiveness, as though he had not acted but had suffered himself to be handled by the infernal powers who had selected him for the victim of their practical joke'. This sounds—as we shall see—very like Meursault's plea that the shots his revolver discharged into the Arab's inert corpse were as many knocks on the door of his undoing. Before long Jim can claim that it was not so much that he 'jumped' as that the others 'willed' him into the lifeboat 'as plainly as if they had reached up with a boat-hook and pulled me over.'

Marlow is well aware that he is being 'bullied', that his sensibilities are being manipulated. He notes that even in his anguish Jim is 'watchful of the effect'. But like Meursault, Jim is not in fact speaking to any one man in particular; Marlow realized that 'he was only speaking before me, in a dispute with an invisible personality, an antagonistic and inseparable partner of his existence—another possessor of his soul.' And just as Meursault's case cannot properly be argued before the assizes, Jim's preoccupations 'were issues beyond the competency of a court of inquiry.' But in the first instance, it is the unknown reader who is convinced; in the second, it is a senior colleague who, long after the hero has gone, survives to argue the extenuating circumstances and, like the traditional chorus of a tragic play, to point out how the retribution eventually exacted infinitely outweighed the original offence.

In winning Marlow over Jim can draw upon all the emotional resources available to a passionate young man engaged in an after-dinner tête-à-tête with a well-disposed listener. Meursault cannot exploit this particularly auspicious situation; but he does have at his disposal the varied rhetorical devices of the literary language, prominent among which is the possibility of considerable discretion over the choice of tenses. In the next section I explore in some detail the manner in which Meursault exercises this discretion within the general framework of his fictional rhetoric—and through him the novelist exerts on the reader the full range of his skills of persuasion and even of cajolery in imposing his particular view of things.

III

The first word in *The Outsider* is 'aujourd'hui' ('Today Mother died'), and although this is at once qualified by the words 'Or perhaps yesterday, I don't know', we have a strong feeling of present time which continues throughout the first two paragraphs. I shall use the term 'dramatic present' to designate this impression, which is not always necessarily provoked by a majority use of the present tense itself—in fact the tense-count in this passage, excluding quotations, and one conditional, gives the following totals: the present tense occurs four times, the perfect six, the imperfect also six, and the future tense eight.

The third paragraph opens with a perfect tense (*passé composé*), 'I took the two o'clock bus', and constitutes one of the major time-breaks of the novel; but because this French tense is ambiguous in the manner we saw earlier, the reader is not immediately aware that Meursault has shifted radically from his stance 'on top of the event' in the first two paragraphs to a position more removed in time. How far removed, the reader does not yet know: the *passé composé* would naturally be used by a speaker to narrate even remote occurrences, and it is this informal address which characterizes Meursault's style: in abandoning the traditional preterite or *passé simple* tense in favour of the more colloquial *passé composé*, Camus introduced a stylistic innovation into French narrative prose. He did so not only to give Meursault's account a conversational immediacy which would make the reader more sympathetic towards him, but also—more importantly—because of the temporal ambiguity of the perfect tense. Thus he killed two birds with one stone: he gave Meursault the accents of Everyman, *and* he was able to keep the reader in doubt as to when the story was composed. The first two paragraphs are fraught with ambiguity and indeed deceit on this last point: the use of the future tense in particular ('I'll catch the two o'clock bus . . . I'll return tomorrow evening') artificially but effectively situates the narrative between the mother's death and her funeral. With the third paragraph, however, we are withdrawn imperceptibly into a structure of more leisurely, distanced narration. The use of the preterite would have made this break crudely evident; the *passé composé* permits a smooth and virtually unnoticed shift.

It is some while, in fact, before the reader becomes aware that Meursault is not temporally on top of the events he describes. Several pages pass before the true perspective is hinted at, in sentences like 'But now I suspect that I was mistaken about this' (p. 21), or 'I can recall' (p. 21), and in the remark that 'other memories of the funeral have stuck in my mind' (p.26). Even an apparently innocent comment like 'I don't care for Sundays' (p.29) performs a deliberate function in keeping the time-scale ambiguous. By the end of the second chapter, however, it is becoming clearer that something unusual is taking place over the perspectives: the remark 'really, nothing in my life had changed' (p.32) is as ironical in the light of what is in fact known to the narrator, as it is typical of the techniques of all suspense-creators who wish to lull the reader into complacency before springing some startling information on him when he least expects it.

The third chapter returns to the 'dramatic present' with the word 'today' ('*Today* I had a busy time in the office', p. 33), but we slip immediately, and as imperceptibly as before, into past time ("There was a pile of bills of laying waiting on my desk and I had to go through them all'). Shortly afterwards there is a third occurrence of the dramatic present in the story about Salamano's dog ('the spaniel *is* an ugly brute . . . You *can* see them in the rue de Lyon . . . ', p. 34). As the animal disappears soon afterwards, it is obvious that this section also is narrated 'on top of the events'. The same applies to the description of Raymond ('the general view hereabouts *is* that he's a pimp', p.35) which, together with a remark or two shortly after ('He, too, has only one room') constitutes a fourth and a fifth occurrence of the dramatic present. It is significant, however, that in these last three cases (Salamano's dog, Raymond and Raymond's flat) the remarks are descriptive and not narrational as they were at the opening of Chapters 1 and 3; nonetheless they serve to maintain the ambiguity about when the account was written which it is obviously important to sustain in this first part of the novel. The effect is continued by the opening sentences of Chapters 4 ('I had a busy time in the office throughout the week') and 5 ('Raymond rang me up at the office'), where once again the *passé composé* leaves it open whether the narration is conducted close to the events described, or at a remove from them. Meursault is thus using a shrewd blend of the dramatic present and the ambiguous past to create an illusion both of immediacy and of objective veracity.

It is not until the fifth chapter that we are given some 'back perspective' on Meursault's existence *prior* to the main events which make up the novel ('As a student I'd had plenty of ambition . . .', he says, and 'I told her I'd lived in Paris for a while . . . ', pp. 48-49), since he is now preparing the reader for the moment when he will show his hand and reveal far more awareness of the implications of his existence and actions than, for rhetorical reasons, he has been willing to do up till now. In passing, he uses a device, favoured by Conrad, Flaubert and others, to blur the temporal boundaries of the narration: free indirect speech; this occurs after the robot-woman has asked him 'if she might sit at my table. *Of course she might*', he adds (p.49). Meursault is frankly disingenuous when he states (p.50) 'but I soon forgot about her'—he remembers her now well enough, and in any case she appears at his trial. And then—after the back perspective, free indirect speech and the mendacious comment just noted—he is ready at last to come clean about the question of when he is writing. 'I answered', he begins, and then adds as if in parentheses, 'why, *I still don't know* . . . ' (p.52). These words, 'je ne sais pas encore pourquoi', lift the narrative right of ambiguous time and situate it in the unambiguous remote past, since they refer to the 'real' present, and reveal that the account is being written with the benefit of considerable hindsight. How much hindsight, the reader still must wait to discover—but this too emerges in due course. For the moment, Meursault is content to hint merely, but he is becoming bolder—witness the overt use of the pluperfect tense in the sentence 'On the previous evening we *had* visited the police station . . .' (p. 53); he is allowing it to be understood that, far from being the passive utterer of a narrative he cannot see to the end of, he is fully aware of its tragic outcome. This pluperfect is followed shortly afterwards by a remark which gives added perspective on the matter: 'For the first time, perhaps, I seriously considered the possibility of my marrying her' (p.55). The effect is discreetly reinforced by a later remark ('probably I was mistaken about this', p.60) which once again reveals an ability to understand after the event.

In the closing pages of the first part of the novel Meursault increasingly pulls out the stops in his rhetoric, and we are treated to a brilliant and eloquent piece of special pleading. The writing, which has up till now been colloquial, restrained and deceptively simple, becomes frankly literary, lyrical and highly-imaged as he seeks to convince us that he did not return to the beach in order to kill (as the prosecution later will argue) but in order 'to be rid of the glare, the sight of women in tears, the strain and effort' and 'retrieve the pool of shadow by the rock and its cool silence' (pp.62-63). He pleads that he 'was rather taken aback' by the sight of the Arab—'my impression had been that the incident was closed, and I hadn't given a thought to it on my way here'. This is the corner-stone of his apologia, the essence of which—like Jim's—is that he was borne along by circumstances beyond his control, such as the fuss and the glare and then the 'shaft of light' from the Arab's blade which seemed to 'scar' his eyelashes and 'gouge into [his] eyeballs' (p.64). In pulling the trigger, he claims, he kills a man only as it were incidentally, because he was really hitting back at the pain which the heat and light were inflicting on him. Once the trigger gave and the revolver had gone off—the use of the more passive form, as with Jim, is of course deliberate—he realized that he 'had shattered the balance of the day', so then ('alors'—the French word is both temporal and causal in meaning) he 'fired four shots more into the inert body' in the wild desperation of his grief and hopelessness—and 'each successive shot', he weeps to relate, 'was another loud, fateful rap on the door of my undoing'. He is doomed; he knows it; but now he has us firmly on his side, because his rhetoric has swayed us so that nothing will be able to shake our conviction of his innocence. A rather taciturn intellectual has thus managed to put forward in writing the case which—aghast at the dishonesty of the venal rhetoric deployed by all round him—he was too weary and powerless to utter verbally in court. The man's reticence—an unwillingness to waste words—as well as his intelligence, are shown repeatedly, for example when Masson wonders how the Arabs had managed to track them to the beach. Meursault uses his brains: 'my impression', he says, 'was that they had seen us taking the bus and noticed Marie's oilcloth bathing-bag' (p. 58), but he makes no attempt to enlighten Masson.

This entire sixth (and last) chapter of the first part is so powerfully written that we notice neither the blatant hindsight (expressed, unusually for Meursault, in the imperfect tense) of the comment about the 'raps on the door of my undoing', nor the literary expertise of the dramatic break in the narrative (between Parts I and II) which immediately follows. The second part opens frankly in the past ('I was questioned several times immediately after my arrest . . . ') and at a much lower level of dramatic tension. Like all good writers, Meursault knows how to work up to a climax, and then cut the narration cleanly before taking it up again in a different key. A musical analogy may help here: this particular break resembles the quiet start of the second movement of Bach's Brandenburg Concerto No. 5, after the intricate frenzy of the harpsichord cadenza has concluded the first movement;

or it can be compared to the short cadence which traditionally ends an Indian raga and releases the tension accumulated during the improvisation of the piece. The calm from such contrasts is essential to our peace. But the effect is highly contrived and certainly one of sophisticated artistry: likewise Meursault is a naïve story-teller only in appearance, a man who masks his eloquence the more effectively to snare us into succumbing to it.

Part II is thus from the outset very different in tone from what precedes it. Meursault intervenes much more in the narration than he was wont to do in Part I. 'It all seemed like a game' (p. 67) is his comment on the proceedings before the examining magistrate, and he retrospectively justifies his passivity as described in the first part by telling his lawyer (and the reader) 'in recent years I'd rather lost the habit of noting my feelings' (pp. 68-69). He also does not hide the fact that he is composing an account ('if I might put it so'—p.69—is a characteristic redactional aside), and he states his motives explicitly now ('I let it go—out of laziness as much as anything else', p.70). When the magistrate asks him 'Why did you pause between the first and second shot?' (p.71) he seems once more to see the red glow hovering over the beach and to feel again the fiery breath on his cheeks, and since it is obvious to him (and to us) that the interrogator would not understand this, he makes no answer. He presents that pause between shots, which so perplexes the magistrate, as a point 'of quite minor importance' (p. 72), a side issue and an irrelevance in the case; *this* he confides to us, who are prepared to agree, but he says nothing to the representative of the Republic. When his interlocutor includes him naturally among 'all the criminals who have come before me', Meursault feels that the concept of his criminality is 'an idea to which I could never get reconciled' (p.74)—and, thanks to the efficiency of his rhetoric, neither can we. For him, and now for us too, the second and subsequent shots were not sadistic but an impersonal, desperate and ultimately insignificant act to which his judges insist on giving sinister meaning. Like many sensitive, introverted and taciturn people, he does not find eloquent words at the right time, but only now, when addressing not a tribunal but unseen readers, does he manage to say the 'something really important' (p.99) of which he longed to unburden himself in court. Even when deeply moved by Céleste's efforts on his behalf he still says nothing and makes no movement, although he feels 'for the first time in my life I wanted to kiss a man' (p.94). The controlled pathos of the entire court scene—in which

Meursault's least actions of the first part (such as taking Marie to a Fernandel picture or accepting coffee at his mother's wake) are systematically interpreted in a manner calculated to cast him in the worst possible light—has us completely on his side: it is a remarkable rhetorical performance, in subtle counterpointed contrast to the conventional eloquence of the legal profession marshalled for and against him. Note how cleverly, for instance, Meursault blurs the distinction between crime and social lapse: the court, of course, is shocked by his 'callousness' not so much because of his 'insensitivity' but rather as a key to his motivations. When he reveals to us how much he responds to nature, he is telling us that he is 'human after all'. It can of course be countered that Meursault could have defended himself similarly in the courtroom, and that his failure to do so is an implied criticism of him by Camus; but this is hardly likely. It is much more probable that Camus shares Meursault's feeling of alienation and therefore lends him his own rhetorical skills which induce us to overlook the fact not only that Meursault has committed murder, but also that he has been more than a little stupid and perverse in making no attempt to defend himself effectively at his trial.

Now that Meursault has us in the palm of his hand, he can afford to slip out of the pretence of being unaware of what is happening to him, and thus can dissipate the ambiguity surrounding the question of the true moment of *rédaction*. He therefore informs us that the preliminary examination of his case lasted 'eleven months' (p. 74) and that 'as time went by' in prison he became resigned to captivity (p.75). The time-scheme of the second chapter in Part II, in fact, is rather complex—Meursault, ranging to and fro over the months in gaol, generalizes about the experience and does not transcribe it in sequence as he had done in Part I. 'On the whole', he concludes, 'I can't say that those months passed slowly' (p.84), and he conveys this impression of generality by an increased reliance on the imperfect tense; in other words, a more normal, traditional pattern of fictional narration begins to establish itself after the dramatic tension of Part I. When he says, speaking of the period before his arrest, 'how long ago it seemed!' (p.98), he is indulging in a poetically licensed lie—it cannot really seem all that long ago or he wouldn't remember it as vividly as the account in Part I reveals he does. For him it cannot, in the nature of things, be remote, but his rhetoric once again has induced *us* to feel its remoteness and the consequent horror of the captivity which causes his life as a free man to appear so distant. In fact, despite his affected indifference to the past ('I've always been far too much absorbed in the present . . . ' p. 101), Meursault reveals a detailed, if selective, recollection—and the selectivity is that of an artist who knows his *métier* and the rhetoric it requires.

The last chapter of the novel begins with another time break: 'I have just refused, for the third time, to see the prison chaplain', which constitutes the sixth and last occurrence (the only instance in the whole of Part II) of the dramatic present. This continues for some nine lines, and then we shift back to the narrated past via the real present ('*I've* no idea how many times I *wondered* . . .', p: 107). Then an unexpected use of the imperfect subjunctive '*eussent*' emphasizes the literary tone of the writing at this point, and conditionals and pluperfects reinforce the impression. We therefore take in our stride, a few pages further on, the dramatic present which introduced the chapter being in its turn relegated to the past: 'It was at one of these moments that I *refused* once again to see the chaplain' (p. 113). This last time-shift—overtly, even blatantly presented—should remove any residual doubts anyone may have that the *entire* novel is narrated from a temporal position well in advance of the outburst against the priest, and even of the rejection of the appeal in which Meursault's last faint hopes of life reposed. He now has nothing more to expect of the 'justice' of men, and as he relives it all through again (p. 120), can concentrate on presenting his defence to the ultimate tribunal, that of his readers. He now awaits the guillotine with calm indifference, even remarking with grim humour that he will be seeing the chaplain again 'quite soon enough' (p. 107). Purged of hope, he can sympathize at the last with his mother, who found happiness with an aged 'fiancé' when her death was imminent. For Meursault also the full realization of his happiness occurs only when he is on the point of losing it. Hence his last stand, and the book we read: an act in vindication of the life he has lived, which he accepted, as in her own way his mother did, and which he proceeds to defend to us his readers. That is why, as Philip Thody writes, 'it is not only at the very end of the novel but all the way through that he is fully conscious that he is right to act as he does'.

To sum up this analysis: there are about six occurrences of the 'dramatic present', all but one in the first part; the 'true present' (that of the *rédaction*) is situated much later in time, most likely after the rejection of the appeal and during the days or weeks leading up to Meursault's execution. The story is narrated principally in the perfect or *passé composé* tense, by definition an 'ambiguous' past tense. There is, in fact, a continual process of temporal expansion and contraction at work, between the event and the close 'dramatic present', and the event and the more distant 'narrative past'. This systole/diastole effect is reinforced by temporal indications like 'I recall . . . ', by dramatic breaks in the flow of the narrative, by redactional asides ('if I might put it so . . . '), by authorial commentary ('It is always interesting to hear oneself being talked about', p. 98), by the skilled deployment of imagery, and above all by the controlled use of pathos. This all adds up to a formidable massing of literary artillery trained on our sensibilities and sympathy, so that long before the Arab's death we are unhesitatingly on the side of the brilliant advocate who portrays himself to us as a harmless individual caught up by a vindictive destiny in a tragic mesh beyond his understanding and control, and so convinces us indubitably of his essential innocence.

IV

We are now in a good position to return to the discussion of the theme which Camus explores through his character's use of tense-shifts and other devices in *The Outsider*. There are three clear phases in Meursault's existence: the years of the student who read books, had ambitions, and lived in Paris: the time of the mature man who is content with humble clerical work because he has come to believe that 'all that was without real importance' (p. 48); and the period of the condemned prisoner who sees even this renunciation in an unfamiliar light. The incoherent emotional explosion of anger at the priest (it is not, we now realize, in the slightest a reasoned statement, for all its literary echoes) occurs because he is exasperated beyond endurance by what he sees as an attempt to waste his time, at a moment when that commodity—of which hitherto he had had an abundance and could afford to be relatively unconcerned about, to the extent of spending many hours with the worthless Raymond—has become a precious (because limited) asset. It is this man—the prisoner aware that every hour counts—who writes (or thinks: the medium itself is not significant) the account we have just read. The book is therefore not a diary, even if—for rhetorical reasons—it seems occasionally to be presented in quasi-journal form; it is in fact *entirely* composed, from beginning to end, in the days or hours which follow the rejection of the prisoner's appeal and the consequential certitude it brings that within a period—which may be long or short but which is surely finite—he will be taken out to die on the public scaffold. In the closing words which puzzled Professor Booth he looks forward with calm anticipation to this event as something indifferent and remote, because he is a man cleansed both of fear and of hope.

How, then, do we see him spending this valuable time? On something which he has at last found to have some 'real importance', we may be sure, otherwise he would not do it. What he is engaged in is nothing short of conducting his trial over again: not the judicial trial in the Algiers assize court, the verdict of which has gone against him and is irreversible, but the trial he is pleading before us, the jury composed of his readers. It is *our* favourable verdict that he is after, and our sympathy which now means more to him than life itself. To obtain that verdict and elicit that sympathy, he is ready to use all the powers of persuasion he has at his command: in other words, he will use the resources of rhetoric, just as the prosecuting attorney did, but in a different, more subtle, and distinctly 'literary' way. He is thus a much more self-conscious and sophisticated narrator—and a more consistent character—than has usually been supposed: he is, in fact, an artist in words, able to manipulate the reader's sympathies with all the verbal dexterity of an expert. Like Esther in *Bleak House* he plays cat-and-mouse with the reader by concealing at the outset the crucial fact that he is writing a story which is over and finished by the time he begins his composition. (Esther's narrative of course lacks the same 'forensic' purpose and so her concealment is less systematically organized; it is, in the nature of things, more of a 'tease'.)

But of course Meursault is not the 'real' artist—the real artist is Albert Camus who, quite consciously and deliberately, lends his creature Meursault the astonishing range of literary skills we have witnessed at work. In both cases, however, it is an excellent example of *ars celare artem*: Meursault gives at first such a powerful impression of near-imbecility that many readers are taken in by it and fall precisely into the trap he lays for them, which is to accept his special pleading as factual, and the prosecuting attorney's rhetoric as a grotesque distortion, an act of flagrant and wilful misunderstanding. But is it? The attorney is doing his job as well as most French lawyers could; anyone who has sat through a murder trial in a French assize court will find nothing out of the ordinary about the business which the accused (and we through him) experiences as terrifyingly unreal. Camus in fact is employing the classic devices of distancing, developed by satirists from Montesquieu and Swift to George Orwell, in order to force his reader to view in an unwholesome and repugnant light things usually taken for granted, and thus to reject as unacceptable what habit (in this case, for the French reader, his own judicial system) has previously conditioned him to accept without question. For always behind Meursault stands Camus, who clearly understood Dostoyevsky's and Kafka's intuitive grasp of the 'outside' man's mentality, despite the fact in this case that the protagonist is no psychopath as in some of Dostoyevsky's novels, and unlike Kafka's K. he is described from within.

Camus therefore uses his creature Meursault as a mask to conceal his own intentions and sympathies, the better to convert us to a way of seeing society whose cruelty and injustice he passionately repudiates—a society in which, as he once eloquently put it, a man may find himself condemned to death for not having wept at his mother's funeral. He was undoubtedly indulging in this early work in a somewhat romantically Manichean attitude towards the problem of social alienation (an attitude provoked not only by awareness of his own deprived social background, but also by his reading of works like *Scarlet and Black* and *Crime and Punishment*), and this led him to force the odds to the extent of risking making Meursault appear an insensitive butcher; it was this aspect of the novel which pained Connolly, and, more recently, Conor Cruise O'Brien. Both critics overlook the fact that however muddled Camus's extra-literary motives might have been at the time, and whatever 'absolute' moral stance one should adopt towards the treatment of the Moorish girl and the murder of her brother, the very difficult rhetorical exercise triumphantly succeeds by virtue of the author's literary skill, so that few readers pause to examine how Meursault has persuaded one jury at least of his complete innocence of the crime for which he is under sentence of death. A cynic might contend that there is therefore no such thing as 'justice', since everything depends on the eloquence of the advocate: Meursault is convicted by a jury when he is defended by a hired lawyer, but he is acquitted by nearly every reader when he undertakes his own defence through the medium of the novel we read. And perhaps the cynic's view was Camus's own, which he was concerned to urge indirectly in this work of narrative prose.

Whatever the truth about that, it is Camus's trick in equipping his hero with the persuasive gift of rhetoric which gives *The Outsider* its justly admired unity as a work of art. But because—necessarily—

the rhetoric is discreetly deployed, and because the case for Meursault is, in appearance at least, implied and understated (in deliberate contrast to the prosecution's, which is emphatic and overstated), critics have tended to be puzzled as to what the novelist is really up to, whereas the common reader is held under the spell produced by the work's consistent unity of inspiration. This spell is cast, as we have seen, by the ageless devices of fictional rhetoric. In not allowing for this, the average critic—who when he engages in critical activity cannot afford to be spell-bound—has tended to overlook a crucial aspect of Camus's art. And it is quite understandable, in a way, that he should: certain books create an effective impression when read as intended, at a sitting, but their devices may well appear inconsistent on closer examination.

As I have already suggested, the most common complaint of inconsistency in *The Outsider* relates to Meursault's character. Camus, the argument goes, present us in Part I with an inarticulate moron who is ineptly transformed, only a few months and a hundred pages later, into an eloquent intellectual whose fluent rhetoric silences even a man of words like the chaplain. The truth, of course, is that in Part I Meursault conceals his understanding so that his fate may appear the more unjust and unfair in retrospect. The analogy which here suggests itself is with the foreshortening of *trompe-l'oeil* scene painting, which from the point of view of the actor on stage is grotesquely distorted and compressed, but observed from the auditorium imitates a vista in depth of tree-lined avenues or of streets bordered by numerous houses. Some effects, indeed, are almost too obvious when seen in close-up, and I think Camus's use of tense-shift in *The Outsider* is a good example of this.

The novel must therefore be accepted as a retrospective attempt to understand, to explain and, above all, to justify Meursault's life and actions. Contrast with this Esther's narrative in *Bleak House:* she also hides her knowledge of the outcome—except for a few forward-looking hints—but she is not out to persuade us of anything, only to narrate a story in as effective (i.e. suspenseful) a manner as possible. To achieve his more urgent aim, Meursault not only exploits the ambiguity of the *passé composé* in the manner we have witnessed, he also indulges on occasion in richly-imaged language of a highly emotive nature so that we are compelled to share with him his revulsion at what he deems to be the patent absurdity of the label of 'criminal'. We have seen, for instance, how acutely he makes us feel his isolation in the court-room, where everyone acts as if the person of least importance in the proceedings, although he is the accused in the case, is Meursault himself. We also respond with him in his sensations of fatigue at the funeral and in the examining magistrate's office, in his unhappiness and deprivation in prison, and in his irrational outburst of fury at the chaplain's interfering solicitude. Long before the jury returns its verdict and sentence has been passed, we are fully won over to Meursault's point of view and reject totally the prosecutor's picture of him as 'an inhuman monster wholly without moral sense' (p. 97).

In the one tribunal from which he is determined to secure an acquittal, indeed, Meursault has prepared his ground so well that the issue is not in doubt. In anguish we watch the prosecution case built up against him, and we too want to protest with Marie that they have 'got it all wrong' (p. 95) since 'no one seems to understand' (p. 96). When Meursault concedes—like Mark Antony slyly eulogizing Brutus only in parentheses—that the prosecuting attorney's 'way of treating the facts showed a certain shrewdness', and made the case against him 'sound quite plausible', we are bound even more firmly to him. Classic injustice, we feel, can always be made to look 'plausible' and nothing Meursault, Marie, Masson or Céleste can say will make any difference, since the court is not prepared to understand how one man may shoot another, even fire four times more into an inert corpse, and still not be guilty of murder. For by this time we are convinced that Meursault's guilt, which he ironically claims to have grasped rather tardily ('for the first time I understood that I was guilty', p. 91), is technical only—in any case, as he is careful to point out, everyone is 'somewhat guilty' in this life—and that what he has committed is an action in self-defence, or at the very worst manslaughter. For the rhetorical trap has been sprung, and we are caught in the web of brilliant advocacy of Meursault's innocence—as he, and his creator Camus, intend that we shall be; as Robert Burden, speaking of *The Fall*, which presents analogies with *The Outsider*, has written: 'the formal rhetorical device of a persuasive confession implicity coerces a more sympathetic response'.

The trial of Meursault for murder in the first degree must thus after all end favourably: we his readers have gladly acquitted him in the assize of the heart and mind, where literary excellence and intellectual prowess are the only effective means of persuasion. We may be sure that it was this *literary* tribunal which mattered most to Meursault, as it mattered most to his creator, and it is the triumph achieved here which will make it possible for him to glory in the expression of hatred that, once he steps on to the scaffold, he expects to hear from the benighted mob, so different from the Stendhalian 'happy few', his readers. Like Raskolnikov in Siberia, it is his chains which make him truly free. And that is why (to adapt the famous words Camus applied, in a similar spirit, to his Sisyphus) we can—indeed we should—imagine Meursault, like Lord Jim at the last, a genuinely happy man.

CHAPTER FOUR

Worlds
Out of Joint

CHAPTER FOUR

Worlds Out of Joint

A man is always a story-teller; he lives surrounded by his own stories as well as those of others. Through them he sees everything that happens to him; and he tries to live his life as if he were fictionalizing it.

SARTRE

I

Sartre's *Nausea* is a remarkably 'significant' novel, even by French standards. So many tendencies meet at the nexus it provides, by virtue not only of its intrinsic nature, but also of the date of its publication: 1938. Ihab Hassan, writing in *New Literary History* (Autumn 1971), considers it a harbinger of post-Modernism, a work (like Beckett's *Murphy*, which appeared the same year) that early on foreshadows — by over a decade—anarchic developments in literature and the arts characteristic of the post-Korean War era. 'If we can arbitrarily state that literary Modernism includes certain works between Jarry's *Ubu Roi* (1896) and Joyce's *Finnegans Wake* (1939), where'—Hassan asks rhetorically—'will we arbitrarily say that post-Modernism begins? A year earlier than the *Wake*? With Sartre's *La Nausée* (1938) or Beckett's *Murphy* (1938)?'

The present chapter examines the way this key novel, *Nausea*, explores extreme situations. It is not necessary for a novel to be great in order to be important: *Nausea,* I shall be arguing, is if anything a rather self-indulgent creation, but, perhaps like no other—not even vastly superior works in the same tradition like *La Condition humaine* or *Voyage au bout de la nuit*—it probes a certain situation characteristic of modern anxieties in a manner equalled only by genius: that of Franz Kafka, a writer working within a different tradition altogether.

75

II

To students and teachers within the necessarily narrower perspective of French literature, *Nausea* is the classic statement of proto-existentialism. The French novel in the nineteen-thirties was torn between metaphysical despair and political commitment; the problem was to be resolved for most writers only in the frank camaraderie of the Resistance movement. All the intellecuals of the period betrayed something of the idealism of that eccentric of genius, Simone Weil, who gave up the relative comfort and security of a teaching post to take a job as an ordinary wage-earner on the factory-floor, martyring herself like any medieval nun; but, true to her vocation as an intellectual, she emerged from the harrowing experience with a book about it. There is something slightly comic in the scourge the French intellectual creates to flagellate himself with, and it was an acute understanding of and sympathy with this occasionally grotesque penchant that led Jean-Paul Sartre to write the novel which in political terms marks the end of the nineteen-thirties. It was his first work of fiction, and was called by the curious title of *Nausea*. Its author was an obscure schoolmaster, a teacher of philosophy, who had hitherto published only theoretical and critical works. He had studied in Germany under the philosopher Heidegger, and had imported into France a loose system of thought which derived ultimately from the Danish nineteenth-century thinker Kierkegaard. It was not long before Sartre himself had developed his own version of this system, which has become known universally as existentialism, because of its cardinal tenet that existence precedes essence. It is not easy for Anglo-Saxons, heirs to the sceptical, empirical, anti-metaphysical British philosophical tradition, to appreciate what was so extraordinary about a statement like 'existence precedes essence.' In classical metaphysics, the essence of a thing is fixed in advance by God, or some all-wise supreme being, and this essence dictates the kind of existence it possesses in the real world. This is a rather abstract notion, but what it means in practice is that man's essence dictates his actions; he is not, therefore, free to decide what he will or will not do. Thus classical thinkers were obliged, unless they found some way out of the impasse, to deny free will.

It was this determinism which the young Sartre vigorously repudiated. It is existence which decides essence, he said (most forcibly in his lecture of 1945, 'Existentialism and Humanism'), not vice versa. In practice, again, he meant that man *is* what he does, that man doesn't simply *do* what he is. In other words, man creates himself by his decisions and actions: none of these decisions and actions is pre-determined for him by his essence. Quite the contrary: man creates his essence by existing, that is, by *doing*. One makes oneself a managing director or philosophy teacher or deck-hand by each one of the thousands of decisions one takes in the course of a life-time, so that at the end one can say—in fact one has to say—'I am what I choose to be'. To deny this fact, and to claim 'I couldn't have done otherwise' or 'circumstances have made me what I am', is to be guilty of what Sartre calls *mauvaise foi*, self-deception, and those who are complacent in that self-deception, like the subjects of the portraits in the Bouville museum, are labelled *salauds*, or 'bastards'.

It is unnecessary to point out that this system of ethics is fraught with theoretical difficulties. For example, it is nonsense to assert that one's every action contributes to making one what one is. When I choose tea instead of coffee for breakfast, am I making a decision little different from the decision whether or not to collaborate with the occupying army of an invading enemy? Sartre in some passages would appear to be saying that the two decisions are of equal ontological significance.

Fortunately it is not my concern to decide on the validity or otherwise of Sartre's moral philosophy, but to examine its effects on his creative writing. Fiction and drama are not vehicles for the weighing up of points of view, but channels of persuasion by which a writer induces us, through the power of his creative imagination, to accept his view of the world or—to borrow Malraux's title—of 'man's estate'. There is little doubt that of the many people who have read and been moved by Sartre's novel *Nausea*, few would consider themselves convinced existentialists, or even know what precisely is meant by the term. What Sartre essentially urges, is a new sense of seriousness and dignity on man. He reacts strongly against Gide's famous *acte gratuit*, or motiveless act, in which (for example) a character murders a complete stranger by pushing him out of a railway carriage, merely in order to demonstrate his independence of cause and effect. Except in so far as a man has already made decisions in the past which affect his present position, says Sartre, he is free of cause but he is not free of effect: what he has decided stands, and commits him irrevocably. Against Gide's apparent frivolity Sartre sets responsibility—that is why he gave his famous defence of his theory the title

'L'existentialisme est un humanisme'. Existentialism gives man the sort of dignity, he claims, that Orestes acquires in his play *The Flies*: the self-respect that comes of having willed an action, and of then accepting it unambiguously as one's own. Orestes kills his mother Clytemnestra along with her lover in revenge for the murder of his father Agamemnon; as a result he must either repent of his action and be forgiven by Zeus, or accept it and draw on himself the plague of flies which has been tormenting the inhabitants of his home town, Argos. His sister Electra (who has urged him against his better judgment to kill the adulterous assassins of their father) now cringes before Zeus's wrath and so escapes the curse of the flies; but Orestes, having taken the plunge and accomplished the deed, proudly takes on the guilt and the curse. He spurns Zeus's offer and departs, followed by the swarm of flies (representing the ancient Greek furies.)

In another of Sartre's plays, *Huis clos* (translated as *'In Camera'* or *'No Exit'*), three people find themselves in hell precisely for not having had the courage of their convictions; their mission now is to torment one another. In probing each other's weaknesses they discover that hell is not a matter of fire and brimstone, even less of devils with red-hot pokers, but a place run with economy of manpower: the damned torture each other mentally. 'Hell', they realize, is 'other people'. Human relationships, in Sartre's thought, are based on such torturer-victim confrontations. In order to preserve what he calls one's 'subjectivity', one 'objectifies' other people. This is the premise of the study written by Sartre's companion and disciple, Simone de Beauvoir, entitled *The Second Sex*, which long before women's liberation argued that man has successfully 'objectified' woman throughout the ages, making her into the sort of subservient, inferior creature who welcomes and accepts her subservience and inferiority, until she is provoked into questioning the confidence trick whereby she has been made to see herself as the 'weaker vessel', and so is led into repudiating the image.

Sartre's neo-Heideggerian philosophy, obscure (and even inconsistent) though much of it undoubtedly is, does render possible a radically new approach to literature and to man. That is why *Nausea* was such an original and important book, when it appeared at the end of the nineteen-thirties. It sounded a completely new note, which had been foreshadowed only by Céline's *Journey to the End of the Night* (1932). It is not without significance that Sartre quotes Céline in the epigraph to his novel. Céline, like Sartre, wrote fiction from a painfully systematic subjective point of view, very different from both the detached elegance of Gide and the impassioned but aloof humanity of Malraux.

In view of this, it is a matter for some surprise that Sartre cast his novel in one of the most hackneyed forms, that of the diary which the 'publisher' claims to have found by accident and which he prints without alteration, a device much used in the eighteenth century, either to pass the fiction off as a true story, or to forestall the accusation that the matter was too licentious for publication, or both. Marivaux, for instance, claims that his *Life of Marianne* is a true story--written down by the heroine herself—the manuscript of which was later discovered and published. Similarly, Laclos pretends that his notorious *Dangerous Liaisons* consists of real letters which genuinely passed between people whose names he has been led to alter merely in order to facilitate publication. Sartre adopts a very similar technique—a 'publisher's note' at the beginning claims that the diary was found among Roquentin's papers and is published as it stands. It is not clear why Sartre did this: he could hardly have thought it would make the story more real. The novel carries its own conviction, which has nothing to do with our believing or not believing in the real existence of Antoine Roquentin; modern fiction has no place for such subterfuges. After this curious beginning the novel continues in the form of Roquentin's diary: we learn all about his everyday existence at Bouville; this is based on Sartre's own experience of life at the big seaport of Le Havre, where he taught before the war. The cold drabness of a French provincial town is vividly conveyed, and the people Roquentin associates with, like Françoise the café-proprietress or the Autodidact, are deftly drawn.

The novel of course is much more than the chronicle of a bachelor's life in a provincial town, where he is working on the life of an eighteenth-century aristocrat. The book is about something else: it describes how a man—an ordinary enough man—comes suddenly to doubt not only the purpose of his existence, but also its very reality. He starts to question the consistency and solidity of material things, and to lose all bearings in the real world. His diary (and that is no doubt the reason for the adoption of the diary form) is his only means of 'keeping tabs' on the world, of not going mad. And it is through the diary—through the *literary act*—that he achieves salvation, the realization that he must create something, even something quite modest like the blues singer's song (Sophie Tucker's *Some of These*

Days), something quite different from the biography of an aristocrat, something which, as he puts it, 'would have to be beautiful and hard as steel and make people ashamed of their existence' (Penguin Modern Classics ed., p.252). It would enable him, as he says, to accept himself, at least retrospectively, and so would confirm his self-discovery. It is an intriguing fact that this self-analysis owes relatively little to the philosophy Sartre was elaborating at the time. It is true that we see 'bastards' in the portrait gallery, and see a victim of 'bad faith' in the Autodidact, but these elements, like Monsieur de Rollebon's atheism, are relatively peripheral and incidental. The central nûb of the plot—how a man suffers a kind of metaphysical concussion and then, slowly coming round, sees life in a new light, is a profoundly original theme which (like Beckett's story, *Molloy*), has its roots more in the unconscious mind than in any consciously elaborated system of ethics. As such it makes *Nausea* the least didactic and most satisfying of Sartre's novels; the unfinished tetralogy *Roads to Freedom*, which began to appear after the war, is a pale achievement when set beside the anarchic youthful vigour of this novel.

The year after *Nausea*, in 1939, Sartre published a collection of short stories, *Le Mur* (known in English as *Intimacy*) which can alone compare with it in quality. They are studies of various pathological states and situations, confirming our impression that *Nausea* has deep psychological roots. The longest, and also the most profound story in the collection is 'The Childhood of a Leader', in which Sartre analyses the rise of the boss mentality, showing the development of the fascist mind from its origins in innocent childhood to its consummation in Jew-baiting. It is a remarkably objective and restrained indictment of the unthinking bourgeois conservatism which could so easily slip into fascism as an evasion. This is an 'existentialist' story only in so far as the embryonic leader settles his own fate by a number of reactions—'decisions' would be too positive a word—to the complex situation which confronts him. To that extent, he is determining his destiny, and so must be held responsible for creating it.

I do not find it very helpful or instructive to read *Nausea*, any more than 'The Childhood of a Leader', as an existentialist work. It naturally bears a relation to Sartre's thinking as adumbrated in other books—just as Camus's *The Outsider* is not unconnected with *The Myth of Sisyphus*—but its roots run deep into his psyche. Simone de Beauvoir tells us, for instance, that he suffered for a time from a particularly unpleasant hallucination; he felt, he says, that he was

being followed along the street by lobsters or crabs. This helps account
for the fact that crustacea occur at least half a dozen times in *Nausea*
and express—like the beetle image which is so disturbing and effective
in Kafka's story *Metamorphosis*—feelings of repulsion and dread. In the
passage I am about to quote Roquentin is running around the docks, in
'absolute panic', until he stops at the water's edge and knows 'a
moment's respite'. It is short-lived; he is suddenly seized with terror
at the thought of what might lie under the calm surface of the black
water:

> A monster? A huge carapace, half embedded in the mud? A dozen
> pairs of claws slowly furrow the slime. The monster raises itself
> a little, every now and then. At the bottom of the water. I went
> nearer, watching for an eddy, a tiny ripple. The cork remained
> motionless among the black spots.
>
> p. 116

Similarly, Roquentin remembers that when he was eight an old man in
the Luxembourg Gardens terrified him because he was sure 'he was
shaping crab-like or lobster-like thoughts in his head' (p. 20). Just as
some people are afraid of spiders—that is, project their psychological
phobias on to these otherwise harmless insects—so Roquentin, and
Sartre standing behind him, is terrorized by crustacea. An equally
intense reaction—this time of disgust and revulsion—is contained in the
sordid phallic imagery which comes naturally to Roquentin's mind.
To express his overpowering sense of something fundamental having
changed, the narrator, like Kafka, uses the symbol of emergence from
sleep. On awakening 'one fine morning' Joseph K. — we learn from
the first sentence of *The Trial*—finds that he has been arrested;
likewise, 'Gregor Samsa awoke one morning from uneasy dreams' to
find himself 'transformed in his bed into a gigantic insect'
(*Metamorphosis*, opening words). Roquentin's sense that the habitual
names will no longer fit familiar things (the kind of epistemological
concussion which Beckett's Watt also experiences) is expressed
however in imagery even more violently sexual than either Beckett or
Kafka would have considered appropriate:

> Somebody who has gone to sleep in his comfortable bed, in his
> quiet, warm bedroom, will wake up naked on a bluish patch of earth,
> in a forest of rustling pricks, rising all red and white towards the sky
> like the chimneys of Jouxtebouville, with big testicles half way out of

the ground, hairy and bulbous, like onions. And birds will flutter around these pricks and peck at them with their beaks and make them bleed. Sperm will flow slowly, gently, from these wounds, sperm mingled with blood, warm and vitreous with little bubbles.

p. 226

A similar phallic image is employed to express Roquentin's disgust at the Autodidact's attempted seduction of the schoolboy in the Public Library: his finger is compared to 'a brown hairy object' approaching, with 'all the grossness (*disgrâce*) of a male organ', the boy's hand, which lies 'on its back, relaxed, soft, and sensual,' looking 'indolently nude', like 'a woman sunning herself on the beach' (p. 234). Such imagery—arising clearly out of masturbation fantasies—contrasts oddly with the matter-of-fact way Roquentin describes his perfunctory, even medicinal embraces with the café proprietress (for example in 'I toyed absent-mindedly with her sex under the bedclothes', p. 88). The guilt feelings which he is careful to exclude from his blasé account of their 'love on an *au pair* basis' (p. 17) is displaced on to other areas: hence Roquentin's preoccupation with perversions of various kinds, such as exhibitionism (p. 117) or the rape and murder of little girls (p. 146) or the Autodidact's pederasty. It is perhaps not immediately clear to the reader of *Nausea* that such displacement is occurring in the novel. Similarly the reader of Kafka's *Metamorphosis* may not perceive at once the subtle intertwining of incest fantasies (Gregor's erotic feelings for his mother, and his consequent fear of his father who, significantly, fatally wounds him with an apple) with masochistic longings (revealed by the frequent allusions to a 'Venus in furs' figure which Gregor has cut out of an illustrated magazine); all this points to a punishment craving closely linked—as Gilles Deleuze has argued this phenomenon usually is—with the Oedipus complex.

III

The 'existentialist' reading of *Nausea* does not take us very far, therefore, in spite of some incidental remarks (such as 'there's nothing, nothing, absolutely no reason for existing', p. 162), which might almost have been planted in the novel to mislead us into interpreting it exclusively on that level. There are, indeed, alternative ways of reading the book: as a unique moment in the development of the novel, for example; not only, as I have suggested, as a throwback to the

eighteenth-century novel, but as a foreshadowing of contemporary
formal experimentalism (the extensive use of what has come to be
called 'intertextuality' is a case in point, and one to which I shall
return), and as a classic of late Modernism in its featuring of jazz in
its 'portrait of the artist as alienated soul' motif, and in its exaltation of
salvation through art. It is remarkable, in fact, for so many currents in
the history of fiction to meet in one work, particularly a first novel, a
book which betrays all the strengths and weaknesses of the type:
naïvety of manner, conventional approach to characterization and
form (as if Joyce, Proust and Virginia Woolf had not already altered all
that), together with an intensity of vision, a success in fixing a mood
which rightly makes it a 'modern classic', and a considerable if
curiously uneven achievement; a work, moreover, totally
representative of its period, as is now, some forty years after, clearly
apparent in retrospect. The contemporary cultural analogues are not
hard to find: I have mentioned Céline already, and the attitude to
women and love projected in Drieu La Rochelle's novels, particularly
Le Feu follet, lies close behind the cynical romanticism (if that is not a
contradiction in terms) of the rather conventional story of Anny in
Nausea; likewise the despair of utterances like 'I haven't a single reason
for living left' (p.233) is equally reminiscent of Drieu's tone. Moreover
even the neo-expressionist landscape of Bouville is characteristic of
attitudes common throughout the period:

Nothing is alive; the wind whistles, straight lines flee into the
darkness The boulevard Noir doesn't have the indecent look of
bourgeois streets, which try to charm the passers-by: it is simply a
reverse side. The reverse side of the rue Jeanne-Berthe-Coeuroy, of
the avenue Galvani. In the vicinity of the station, the people of
Bouville still look after it a little; they clean it now and then because
of the travellers. But, immediately afterwards, they abandon it and it
rushes straight on, in total darkness, finally bumping into the
avenue Galvani. The town has forgotten it. Sometimes a big
mud-coloured lorry thunders across it at top speed. Nobody even
commits any murders on it, for want of murderers and victims. The
boulevard Noir is inhuman. Like a mineral. Like a triangle. We are
lucky to have a boulevard like that at Bouville. Usually you find
them only in capitals—in Berlin near Neukölln or again towards
Friedrichshain; in London behind Greenwich. Straight, dirty
corridors, with a howling draught and wide, treeless pavements.

They are nearly always on the outskirts in those strange districts where cities are manufactured, near goods stations, tram depots, slaughter-houses, and gasometers. Two days after a downpour, when the whole city is moist in the sunshine and radiates damp heat, they are still cold, they keep their mud and puddles. They even have puddles of water which never dry up, except one month in the year, August.

p.43

The oppressive, exclusively urban quality of those 'straight, dirty corridors', threatened with invasion by 'the Vegetation . . . crawling for mile after mile towards the towns . . . waiting . . . to clamber over the stones, . . . grip them, search them, burst them open with its long black pincers' (pp. 221-2), is a curious amalgam of Friedrich Murnau's expressionism and the social pessimism of Marcel Carné. Indeed the release of films like Carné's *Quai des Brumes* and *Le Jour se lève* was almost exactly contemporary with the publication of *Nausea*; they similarly treat of the squalid sufferings of lower-class people, such as Lucie the charwoman of *Nausea* and her tubercular, alcoholic husband. And the attitude to a French provincial Sunday as something painfully to be endured is found not only in this novel but also in Camus's *The Outsider* which followed it a mere four years later.

IV

In this diary record of an alienated imagination the character of the diarist is naturally crucial. Roquentin is a *rentier*, a man for whom 'there is neither Monday nor Sunday' (p.82); a man indeed who has at his disposal an annual income of 14,400 francs (p.245). This *rentier* is a scholar, a man who revels in the delights of literary composition and historical detection:

I had worked all day long in the Mazarine; I had just realized, from his correspondence of 1789-90, the masterly way in which he duped Nerciat. It was dark, I was going down the avenue du Maine, and on the corner of the rue de la Gaîté I bought some chestnuts. How happy I was! I laughed all by myself at the thought of the face Nerciat must have made when he came back from Germany.

p.25

Not unexpectedly this rentier-scholar is an introvert. He rarely talks or smiles, and even when he does smile, it is always for a reason: 'I smile at him. I should like this smile to reveal to him all that he is trying to conceal from himself' (p. 104). And like those who stare a great deal, he is afraid of being caught staring. On one level, therefore, the novel is a brilliant evocation of an introvert's breakdown. He gazes at himself in the mirror:

> The eyes in particular, seen at such close quarters, are horrible. They are glassy, soft, blind, and red-rimmed; anyone would think they were fish-scales. I lean my whole weight on the porcelain edge, I push my face forward until it touches the mirror. The eyes, the nose, the mouth disappear: nothing human is left. Brown wrinkles on each side of the feverish swelling of the lips, crevices, mole-hills. A silky white down runs along the wide slopes of the cheeks, two hairs protrude from the nostrils: it's a geological relief map. And, in spite of everything, this lunar world is familiar to me. I can't say that I *recognise* the details. But the whole thing gives me an impression of something seen before which numbs me.
>
> p.31

It is characteristic of Roquentin's breakdown that frenzied, even hysterical prose alternates with temporary calm. The impassioned entry for a Monday, for instance, is followed by this laconic entry for Tuesday: 'Nothing. Existed' (p. 149). Roquentin's crisis—which reaches its climax in the incident of the chestnut-tree root—is a kind of Laingian collapse, a secular dark night of the soul, resulting in a form of health, certainly a radical rediscovery of self. One is therefore not surprised to find that Roquentin's account, though alert and sharp, is oddly humourless. This is because he is given to satirical comments of the kind: 'you get the impression that their normal condition is silence and that speech is a slight fever which attacks them now and then' (p.76), or: 'when his establishment empties, his head empties too' (p. 16). The whole episode of the Autodidact, at least until the explosion in the Public Library, is strongly satirical. Although we are offered wit of a kind there is, as I have suggested, strangely little humour; perhaps because there is not sufficient distance between Roquentin and his creator, certainly less than between Beckett and his Murphy. It could be argued—although I would not wish to do so—that there is a hint of distancing at the very end of the novel; the narrator's gesture towards writing a novel is put in doubt by the evident fact that the novel was never written, thus undercutting the images of rebirth in the very last paragraph (Hotel *Printania, damp* wood, *rain* over Bouville). But if this is satire by the author at the narrator's expense, the motion is such a velleity as to be virtually imperceptible. It is thus difficult to avoid the conclusion that *Nausea* is, in the final analysis, a self-indulgent book. The curiously negative politics of the work—politics Sartre was later to repudiate—bear this out. Like young rebels of a later period, Roquentin does not shrink from theft (he tells us he stole letters from archives in Moscow). His resentment against the self-assured figures of the nineteenth-century city is unlimited, but he also dislikes the Left, Communists and Catholic humanists alike. His iconoclasm embraces both Guéhenno and Barrès, the liberal as much as the reactionary.

V

It follows from this that the diary which the novel offers us is a narcissistic document, stressing—as Anny does in life—the importance of its 'privileged moments'. Of course, Roquentin's journal is a diary in a rather special sense: really an address to a silent reader; Roquentin goes to some pains to explain his rather eccentric interest in garbage (p.21), or he plays with—and teases—his hearer: for instance, he announces (on p. 30) that Rollebon bores him, but the *reader* isn't bored, on the contrary: these snippets in the book are like lumps of date in a piece of tea-time cake, the pleasant sweetening we all wait for, as Anny turns the pages in search of the pictures in her copy of Michelet's *History of France*. Like the Michelet illustrations the tasty morsels about Rollebon have 'little connnection with the text on the adjoining pages' (p. 209). Roquentin doesn't hesitate to quote the most hackneyed stories ostensibly connected with Rollebon, such as his conversion *in extremis* of the moribund. This is an amusing if much-travelled anecdote, and one feels that Sartre's only justification for including it was that he enjoyed it as such.

The diary is, in fact, something of a sham. The editorial notes which grace the first few pages are extraordinarily naïve: there is no need for the editors to pretend to any doubt that the undated sheet precedes the start of the diary proper, since there is clear evidence that this is the case—not least that on 30 January Roquentin talks about handling a pebble 'the other day' (p. 22); the pebble is referred to in the undated sheet (p.10). To clinch the matter, we have only to note that Roquentin talks about a 'false alarm' on 29 January (p. 13), clearly referring to the 'disgust' he felt on the seashore when he tried to play 'ducks and drakes' alongside the children (pp.10-11).

Roquentin narrates most episodes in the present tense, but it is clear that this is a kind of dramatic present, since he often 'writes up' the incidents some hours after their occurrence: he uses the present tense in as self-consciously rhetorical a fashion as Meursault uses the past indefinite tense. Some of his entries are long—almost short stories in their own right—and some are very brief, taking up a single line. There is evidence that the diary-form breaks down towards the end in any case, as if Sartre were losing interest in this artificial form of narrative: it was certainly convenient for Roquentin's 'editors' that this manuscript ended on the impressive note about rain on Bouville, and not, as it might well have done, in mid-sentence. In fact, the whole book is a highly-wrought artefact. Sartre is particularly adept at ironic counterpoint, for instance in confronting the 'official' portrait of Blévigne with the unofficial one published in a satirical newspaper (pp. 134-5). The most extended example of this is the quotation from Balzac's *Eugénie Grandet*. This 'intertext' serves many purposes. It subtly reminds us that Roquentin, like Eugénie, pins his hopes on the return of a long-lost lover. It also constitutes, in a contemporary situation of chaos, a reference to the solidity of a cultural past, a literary tradition of stable values. Moreover, in striking an archaic note, it comments ironically on the social situation observed by the narrator in the restaurant where he is reading the book; even when he has left the restaurant, there is a kind of prolongation of the Grandet family situation—a sort of reflection-echo—in the three people he observes leaving for their Sunday walk:

> I walked along the quiet rue Bressan. The sun had scattered the clouds and it was fine. A family had just come out of a villa called 'The Wave'. The daughter was buttoning her gloves out on the pavement. She could have been thirty. The mother, planted on the first of the flight of steps, was looking straight ahead with an assured expression, and breathing hard. Of the father I could see only the huge back. Bent over the keyhole, he was locking the door. The house would remain dark and empty until they got back.

p.77

There are other literary and sub-literary quotations in the text: a brand of cigarettes is known as 'Salammbô', for instance, and the Vicar of Wakefield is possibly being referred to obliquely in the person of Dr. Wakefield (p. 129). At the sub-literary level, there are characteristically hyperbolic quotations from the local newspaper, which serve to emphasize the traditional quality of provincial life reflected in the novel. Although all of this looks forward to the manner of Claude Simon and other contemporary novelists, we should not confuse the two; Simon's recent works are almost collages, built up of a number of heterogeneous 'intertexts' ranging from cigar labels to the transcript of the proceedings of a Writers' Congress. Although *Nausea* points in this direction, it is far from being a collage novel itself. It operates by more traditional methods: by symbolism, for instance (the name of the 'rue des Mutilés', p. 10, hints that Roquentin is mutilated psychologically); by oxymoron ('I'm afraid of towns. But you musn't leave them', p. 221); and by metaphor, such as the curious instance of Roquentin's feeling 'pregnant' with Rollebon:

> A little earlier he was there, inside me, quiet and warm, and now and then I could feel him stirring. He was quite alive, more alive to me than the Autodidact or the manageress of the Rendez-vous des Cheminots. Admittedly he had his whims, he could stay for several days without giving any sign of life; but often, on mysteriously fine days, like the man in a weather-box, he would put his nose out and I would catch sight of his pale face and his blue cheeks. And even when he didn't show up himself, he weighed heavily on my heart and I felt full up.
>
> p.140

This figurative patterning even affects the nausea, which comes and goes. Roquentin feels no disgust at the idea of the sweaty American writing the jazz tune in the torrid heat of a New York summer, whereas there is something almost gothick about this image inspired by the thought of a red rag blown by the wind:

> When the rag gets close to him he will see that it is a quarter of rotten meat, covered with dust, crawling and hopping along, a piece of tortured flesh rolling in the gutters and spasmodically shooting out jets of blood.
>
> p. 226

The truth is that Roquentin is attempting to fictionalize his own experience. He is 'as happy as the hero of a novel' (p.82), and yet warns himself about the danger of succumbing to the sublime, to 'literature' (p. 85); there is something unintentionally comic about his thus reminding himself of his distrust of literature while enjoying the feeling of being a fictional character. Gradually, of course, the idea grows in his mind that he should himself write a novel. He begins by thinking that he would do better to use his accumulated material on Rollebon in fictional form, but at the very end he decides against this, and contemplates 'another kind of book . . . the sort of story . . . which could never happen, an adventure' (p. 252). Such literary aspirations are ironic in the light of the fact that Sartre was later to lose all faith in writing fiction at all.

VI

Nausea is a curiously neo-symbolist novel, then, harking back to the *fin-de-siècle* belief that language aspires to the condition of music. It is, at the same time, a surrealist work, in which the surrealism is not fully integrated, as in this strange quotation:

> Somebody else will feel something scratching inside his mouth. And he will go to a mirror, open his mouth: and his tongue will have become a huge living centipede, rubbing its legs together and scraping his palate. He will try to spit it out, but the centipede will be part of himself and he will have to tear it out with his hands.

p. 266

One thinks immediately of Kafka's *Metamorphosis*. But in that great story, the beetle image is fully integrated in the myth: it is a dream that is not a dream, a nightmare conducted with remorseless logic. *Nausea* is a more transcendental work, almost neo-Platonic in the sense in which A.E. Dyson uses the term in an essay on *The Trial*: 'man moves in the world as an alienated being, cut off from his true life, yet as much the agent of his catastrophe as its victim'. But Kafka—for whom man was a 'suicidal notion forming in God's mind'—is an altogether more astringent author than Sartre. In Kafka's absurd universe man is blindly punished, the rigour of that necessity contrasting cruelly with the grotesque contingency of the world. His universe is one place 'where no assumption is safe, no technique works, no person can be trusted, no development can be "placed" or understood' (Dyson). It is for this reason that the first sentence or two of his stories—such as 'It was late in the evening when K. arrived. The village was deep in snow. The Castle hill was hidden, veiled in mist and darkness, nor was there even a glimmer of light to show that a castle was there'—are the clearest statements the reader is ever to be offered. Sartre's terrors are limited by the fact that the real world is preserved: a chestnut-tree root writhes in a park in a provincial town in northern France. For all *Nausea's* aesthetic gothicism, therefore, it does not take us beyond the realm of the familiar: Sartre's gamble, through Roquentin, seems disturbingly tainted with 'bad faith', and his portrayal of a 'world out of joint' appears a self-indulgent fantasy when compared with the remorseless bleakness of Kafka's demonstration of the collapse into comic horror of his heroes' universe of cosy flats and easy jobs.

CHAPTER FIVE

A Choice of
Nightmares

CHAPTER FIVE

A Choice of Nightmares

We live, as we dream—alone . . .

CONRAD

I

There is a real sense in which we are all creators of fiction even if we have never written a line of imaginative prose. All human beings dream: mostly during the hours of darkness, but also at odd times during the day. Usually these dreams are problem-solvers, in which with a greater or lesser degree of fantasy we extricate ourselves from the difficulties and conflicts of everyday life; others are pure wish-fulfilment, or 'castles in Spain.' But others, again—and usually the most striking—are subtle, complex fictions in which we tell ourselves a story, or 'show' ourselves a film. We carry about with us, in fact, our own 'Inflight Motion Pictures' system, and the programme, different each time, flickers in full technicolor on the inner screen of our consciousness soon after our take-off into sleep. We are fortunate if we can remember much about these dreams afterwards: for the most part they are lost irretrievably, like the stories we were told in childhood and have all but forgotten. Sometimes a particularly memorable incident sticks in our mind, an especially piquant event or colourful encounter: for those fictions which we create spontaneously and artlessly for ourselves are often as exciting as any book.

The present chapter deals therefore with the more subterranean forces at work in the novel by looking at fiction as if it were a kind of structured dream—but a dream the novelist shares with the reader, a dream transcending the personal concerns of a particular individual and reaching out to involve the reader also.

93

II

Dreams, of course, especially since Freud, have been the concern of the psychologist; and, not surprisingly, psychologists have been attracted to literature as to a fabulously abundant repository of recorded, structured dreams, just as literary critics have turned to psychology in the hope of providing themselves with a methodology which they can use in the analysis and elucidation of works of the imagination, especially the more difficult, arcane, symbolic fictions we associate with Modernism.

In itself, however, psychology is no new thing in literature. It has always been an area of activity for the creative writer, seen as a kind of amateur analyst of conscious or semi-conscious feelings, thoughts or attitudes. The term 'psychological fiction', for instance, covers some of the greatest of all novels, like James's *Portrait of a Lady* or Flaubert's *Madame Bovary* or Tolstoy's *Anna Karenina*, and 'psychological drama' includes such penetrating analyses of human emotions as *Hamlet* and *Faust* and *Hedda Gabler*. But psychology in this sense—meaning the exposure, dissection and acute appraisal of the mind and mood of a fictional but representative human character by a privileged observer—has tended to give ground as a critical term in favour of a more scientific sense drawing its inspiration from the development of psychoanalysis by Sigmund Freud and of analytical psychology by C.G. Jung. The writings of these two men and of their disciples have exerted a profound influence on literary criticism, partly because they were themselves so literate and cultivated, ever-ready to seek their examples and even their terminology within the domain of the creative arts in general, and literature in particular: Freud gave the name of the protagonist of Sophocles's *Oedipus Rex* to what he saw as 'the nuclear complex of the neuroses', and Jung listed Schiller's essay on naïve and sentimental poetry and Nietzsche's *Birth of Tragedy* among the antecedents of his treatise on *Psychological Types* (the 'introverted' and the 'extraverted'). This pioneering study, like Freud's *Interpretation of Dreams* (1900), has suggested an approach to works of the imagination which pays close attention to unconscious motivations and feelings, either on the part of the author (as in Michel Butor's essay on the poet Baudelaire), or within a well-known fictional character (as in Ernest Jones's Freudian analysis of Hamlet). Creative writers themselves have inevitably been influenced by the revelations of psychological investigation: works as different as *The Sound and The*

Fury by William Faulkner and Albert Camus's *The Outsider* bear witness to this, as well as a host of lesser books like J.D. Salinger's *Catcher in the Rye* or Philip Roth's selfconsciously psychoanalytical novel *Portnoy's Complaint*.

The central *logical* problem with which scientific psychology has to wrestle—that the 'unconscious' cannot be observed as such and so cannot be demonstrated by the usual standards of verification to exist—is not necessarily a difficulty for the literary critic, who can treat the unconscious as a formal concept or working hypothesis, rather than as a causal entity. Writers can be seen as betraying unconscious conflicts (e.g. Baudelaire's resentment of his mother's second marriage, or Kafka's ambivalent relationship with his father) or, more subtly, as sublimating these feelings in their works in much the same way as we all refract anxieties and frustrations by means of arcane imagery in our dreams.

An example of this sublimation at work is the way conflicts of great violence are acted out and purged in *Wuthering Heights*. In this great imaginative novel Catherine's well-remembered cry—'I *am* Heathcliff'—is characteristic of the kind of libidinal circularity which typifies incestuous eroticism. The intensely phallic nature of this eroticism is underlined by Lockwood's dream which is described in these terms:

> I began to dream, almost before I ceased to be sensible of my locality. I thought it was morning; and I had set out on my way home, with Joseph for a guide. The snow lay yards deep in our road; and, as we floundered on, my companion wearied me with constant reproaches that I had not brought a pilgrim's staff: telling me that I could never get into the house without one, and boastfully flourishing a heavy-headed cudgel, which I understood to be so denominated.
>
> For a moment I considered it absurd that I should need such a weapon to gain admittance into my own residence.

Penguin English Library ed., pp. 64-65

The significance of the 'heavy-headed cudgel' with which one will seek to gain admittance into one's own 'residence' needs no elaboration. This kind of imagery is easily comprehensible in terms of the circumstances in which Emily Brontë, evidently a highly-sexed and firmly-repressed parson's daughter, grew up, one of three daughters in an isolated family and in close intimacy with a brother. But such a reading of the book in narrowly Freudian terms would not only rely with naïve insistence on biographical information, it would also commit the 'fallacy of the single factor', a fallacy which I shall discuss later. Any thoroughgoing Freudian interpretation of *Wuthering Heights* is obliged to dismiss the end of the book as novelettish, which is not the way most readers have taken it:

> My walk home was lengthened by a diversion in the direction of the kirk. When beneath its walls, I perceived decay had made progress, even in seven months—many a window showed black gaps deprived of glass; and slates jutted off, here and there, beyond the right line of the roof, to be gradually worked off in coming autumn storms.
>
> I sought, and soon discovered, the three head-stones on the slope next the moor—the middle one, grey, and half buried in heath— Edgar Linton's only harmonized by the turf and moss, creeping up its foot—Heathcliff's still bare.
>
> I lingered round them, under that benign sky; watched the moths fluttering among the heath and hare-bells; listened to the soft wind breathing through the grass; and wondered how anyone could ever imagine unquiet slumbers, for the sleepers in that quiet earth.

Most readers have found this end satisfying and soothing, as representing the final resolution of all the conflicts which have tugged and destroyed the protagonists: the mystery and richness of the novel resides in the fact that it does, to a large extent, resolve the tensions it creates. The same applies in the case of *Moby Dick*, another great psychological epic of the struggle between good and evil, god and devil, self and anti-self. The abrupt ending leaves the witnessing-angel figure of Ishmael (who has a charmed existence) alive but 'orphaned', the fate of the divine father-figure (Moby Dick) uncertain, but at least the elimination of the Promethean-devil figure (Ahab) assured. At great cost and after a fierce struggle, which may have destroyed (as it has evidently wounded) the paternal goodness itself, the wicked (or merely rebellious) principle is vanquished. A piece of literature like these can be said to effect an exploration, even a restless probing, of unconscious problems—as a dream may do, in a less structured manner—and so should be viewed as a form of self-therapy and as evidence, not of neurotic sickness as Freud in his more naïve moments tended to assert, but of mental health.

III

One area, too, where useful work can be done on psychology and the
creative imagination is in significant forms of minor literature, such as
detective fiction. With Georges Simenon, for instance, we are
intrigued by the fact that his villains tend to be *petit-bourgeois rentiers*
who turn to crime as they go to seed. This reveals an attitude to evil on
Simenon's part which is probably only half-conscious. The good
people in his novels are usually humble: barmaids, seamen, the
traditional hewers of wood and drawers of water. Does Simenon, one
wonders, feel an obscure guilt about his social condition? Is that why
he makes his own kind, the stay-at-home middle class *pantouflard* into
murderers, and those who serve them—maids and their lowly
boyfriends—into victims saved by Maigret at the eleventh hour from
unjust accusation engineered by those same clever *petite bourgeois?* Is
he soothing feelings of guilt at being an exploiter himself? Is Maigret
an idealization of himself, someone who—unlike Simenon, who can only
sit at home and write books—is efficient, gruff, no-nonsense, gets his
man in the end and reveals to an impressed circle (it is significant, I
think, that Maigret's *dénouements* tend to be staged like royal
audiences) the low-grade felonies of which his tight-lipped
'respectable' people are capable? Is that why Simenon, a pipe-smoker,
has made Maigret the same, so that for us he is inseparable from his
briar and his simple workman's smoking mixture, the inexpensive
tabac gris? Is Maigret an imaginary, immensely admired elder brother
for Simenon? Is that why Maigret is so loveable, for all his taciturn
boorishness? Has Simenon injected into Maigret, largely for
unconscious reasons, a strong emotive charge, in compensation for his
own social guilt? It may not be possible to give definite answers to
these questions, but it is, to say the least, curious that so much of
Simenon's work is set in dusty, spacious bourgeois apartments which
have seen better days, and that his milieu is oddly restricted to a small
social group. He writes novels out of a kind of mania for order, and
(literally) sweats over them:

> I write novels because I need to go out of my own skin. I prefer not
> to analyse myself too much. It's not good to know oneself very well
> . . . I stay three or four hours here, typing, and then take a shower,
> and change all my clothes because they're completely wet . . . When
> a novel is on its way, I don't enjoy it at all. I suffer very much. I take

people at the end of themselves, and to be in the skin of such people for a week is very tiring. So when it's finished, I go all round the house and I say: 'Finished! Everyone, it's finished!'

The Listener, 20 March 1969

It is clear from this that writing for Simenon is a compulsive act of sublimation, an activity in which he purges himself of his phantoms. There are, of course, other creative enterprises in popular culture which act more collectively, as fictions working out shared myths and obsessions: comic strips and television serials are an obvious case. Most of these originate in the United States, and must be seen as the self-reflection of middle America, betraying its presumptions and secret anxieties. As good an example as any is the animated comic-strip shown widely on television networks around the world, *The Flintstones*.

Because *The Flintstones* is a cartoon serial, with no live actors except for the voice parts, it relies more than most soap-operas on simplified caricatures. Two couples are featured; they are aged about forty, have clearly been married for some time and are friends and neighbours. Wilma lives with Fred and Betty with Barney. The men are rather corpulent; Fred, the taller, is dark-haired, and Barney is short and fair. Of the wives, Wilma is the fair one and Betty the brunette; both are slim and well groomed. They dominate their respective husbands, who are rather afraid of them: several episodes concern escapades in which the men succeed by some boyish subterfuge or other in taking an evening off away from their wives. Across the marriage barrier there is also a dominant pair: Betty is a weaker personality than Wilma and Barney is exploited by Fred, a not very intelligent bully. Barney is the one who has all the bright ideas which Fred proceeds to take over as his own; but being the impatient type he often makes a fool of himself by his impulsive and unreflecting actions.

These people are thus presented to us as a very ordinary American middle-class quartet. The serial's particular 'gimmick' is to set them in prehistoric Stone Age times. So everything in the consumer durables line is made of stone—even the television set. Just as Tom and Jerry transpose the cat and mouse situation into a quasi-human context, the Flintstones update and Americanize paleolithic man. Both families, for example, possess a motor car, even if its wheels are of stone and its chassis is made of wood; the one-storey houses they live in (with garden at the back) are hollowed out of boulders. The time clock which checks Fred into work is a dinosaur which perforates his card with its teeth; and the family cat is a household-size sabre-toothed tiger. The vacuum cleaner is a baby elephant, the shower is provided by courtesy of a mastodon's trunk, and so on. As with *Astérix*, much of the humour arises from the deliberate and knowing exploitation of anachronism.

The attitude to sex is nervously orthodox. Fred and Barney are respectably married men, afraid of the 'chicks'. An all-male night out at the bowling alley is their ideal of fun. The wives are equally close friends. It is the nature of relationships *between* the sexes which is left vague: the men do things together, the women likewise. They may well go out as a foursome, but rarely as separate couples. The younger generation, with their 'groovy' parties and wildly erotic behaviour, are an object of uneasy curiosity to the men. Wilma and Betty, for their part, are unruffled, untousled and vaguely menacing dolls.

On the socio-economic level the serial is equally revealing of middle-class attitudes. One episode is concerned with some of the trappings of middle-income living: building a swimming pool by do-it-yourself methods and holding barbecue parties around it. (A sensitive spot was touched upon here, in that the neighbours agree to share the pool by building it across their boundary; the inevitable frictions which result are only resolved by the timely intervention of the wives). Although by no means deprived, the people featured in the strip are not wealthy either: Fred works in a quarry, driving a dinosaur-excavator, and has the burly physique, loud voice and uncouth manners which the creators of the serial clearly associate with manual workers in heavy industry. Fred sometimes finds himself a bit short of ready cash, and the fear of being fired continually haunts him. To this is added the menace of conformity: when as a result of a blow on the head Fred becomes 'cultured', interested in opera and modern art, the neighbours organize a persecution campaign. Happily for Fred—and even more for his greatly puzzled wife—another blow restores him to his familiar gross normality.

Of course the story is fantasy, with the requisite 'biffings' and 'bashings' of the genre, the falling in and out of friendship of the protagonists, with no real harm done and all sorted out happily at the end. But underneath the straightforward appeal to overgrown schoolboys is both a folk-myth which sublimates anxieties about redundancy in a world in which people indulge in conspicuous consumption to the very limit of their income, and a parable which soothes envy of the allegedly highly-sexed younger generation. The serial brings comfort by reflecting, and thus reinforcing, social codes and attitudes (especially those of conformity and respectabilty) by which middle America lives and attempts to preserve itself.

But if popular television is a revealer of the unconscious cultural assumptions of the class for which it is created, there is the interesting phenomenon of 'camp' in which legendary figures of popular culture like Batman and James Bond become a cult at a second remove, avidly followed by people who are well aware of the 'unconscious' fantasies about virility, domination and power to which such fictions pander. Joseph Losey's film *Modesty Blaise* simultaneously 'sent up' the espionage genre and extended its repertoire. Such developments—some recent science fiction is another case in point—indicate both a sophisticated awareness among the mass public of a generalized loss of belief in the old hero myths, and a readiness to join in the nostalgic celebration of the values these used to represent.

IV

The manner in which unconscious tensions predispose certain forms of imaginative writing at the individual level can be seen clearly in Albert Camus's first novel, *The Outsider*, already discussed at some length, though from a rather different point of view, in Chapter 3. In what follows now I should make it clear that I am not attempting to psychoanalyse the man Albert Camus on the basis of his writings, nor his characters on the evidence of their behaviour: I hope thereby that I shall avoid the naïve excesses of some so-called 'psychocriticism'. In particular, I do not accept Charles Mauron's assumption that the 'unconscious' personality of the implied author and of the biographical author are one and the same. I believe one can avoid psychoanalysing a character (and its creator by implication) by concentrating on formal aspects of the work. We say to ourselves, in reading a literary work, these factors are, *prima facie*, puzzling. If a particular psychological theory can account for them in a satisfying way we are entitled to use it, without implying anything about the author; him we see as a complex person, able to act as a sounding-board and not necessarily himself the victim of any neurosis or conflict. We can thus avoid what B.A. Rowley has termed 'the fallacy of the single factor' and 'the fallacy of fundamentality', which he sees as the twin pitfalls of this form of critical analysis. Thus I shall not claim of *The Outsider* that the Oedipal situation is the sole or even the most profound element in the novel, but only one factor operating within the resonances which the work provokes in us. And although such exegetical activity is not in itself evaluative—as I myself have just shown, in devoting more space to a piece of popular entertainment, *The Flintstones,* than to one of the great novels of the English language, *Wuthering Heights*—the application of psychological theory to the understanding of the formal indications within a work can take us quite a long way towards evaluation. The aesthetically satisfying cannot, in other words, be defined in terms of psychology, although it is likely that a great work of art will be psychologically complex, and certain that it will project at an unconscious level those universal myths of tension, conflict and resolution by which we live. Both of the novels I shall now analyse in some depth are great works of art by any standard. The approach is not the same in both cases, however. *The Outsider* is subjected to a fairly orthodox Freudian reading, Samuel Beckett's *Molloy* is discussed in terms of the sadomasochistic syndrome. But the two novels are not entirely unrelated. *Molloy* begins with these sober words: 'I am in my mother's room. It's I who live there now'; and in *A Happy Death,* Camus's first attempt at a novel on the outsider theme, we read: 'He slept in what used to be his mother's room . . .' In fact, since Sartre's early 'explication' of *The Outsider* in terms of a classical, orderly work composed about and against the Absurd, close in manner and intention to a *conte* by Voltaire, critics have returned again and again to this seemingly most straightforward of novels, so clearly in the austere tradition of French fiction which stems from *The Princess of Cleves,* and yet so individual and unique: for never again was Camus to achieve the same perfect amalgam of mythic power and formal rigour.

It is therefore not surprising that critics have moved beyond Sartre's description. They have explained *The Outsider* in terms of a confrontation between mother and son, of maternal and paternal values, or of sea and sun. Without wishing to quarrel with any of these analyses, I feel that they do not press their conclusions far enough. So far as I know, Alain Robbe-Grillet (in *Towards a New Novel*) is the only critic to have stated unambiguously that Meursault's revolt as expressed in *The Outsider* has passional roots:

> The absurd is simply a form of tragic humanism. It is not a statement of separation between man and objects. It is a lover's quarrel, leading to a crime of passion. The world is accused of being an accessory to murder.

Robbe-Grillet here implies that Meursault's reaction to the absurd is not
only philosophical, but also psychological. This hint throws light on much
of Camus's writing, to the complexity of which critics have not really done
justice. This is especially true of 'The Renegade', the short story in
Exile and the Kingdom which is apparently considered to be so
untypical of its author as not to repay close study; for although one
critic, Philip Thody, has devoted some attention to it, even he has not
properly understood its plot. I believe that 'The Renegade', first
published in 1956, is an extraordinary document which reveals much
about Camus's art and so helps us to see *The Outsider* in a fresh light.
The central event in this story about a European taken captive by a
primitive tribe, is the cutting out of the hero's tongue after he has
been led to make a compromising gesture to a woman who seems to be
offering herself. The prisoner's desires have been inflamed 'as a result
of being present, almost every day, at that impersonal and nasty act
which I heard without seeing it', that is, the ritual rape of the woman
by the sorcerer. The barbarous mutilation leaves a 'black dried hole
that no muscle of live flexible flesh revives now', stuffed with 'a gag of
strange-smelling dry grasses'.

The story has of course a philosophical theme connected with the
ethical problem of good and evil, of the powerlessness of love against
hatred, which clearly links it to *The Plague*: the hero, who has absconded
from a seminary in Algiers with the treasurer's chest and thrown off his
habit, arrogantly presumes to brave the heathen alone, unaided by the
comforts of the church. He later wishes to implicate the whole of
western civilization in his own downfall, and on the arrival of the
official chaplain murders him. Having been defeated by the greater
strength of evil through overestimating his own steadfastness, he thus
turns renegade, and worships what he cannot destroy: it is as if Dr.
Rieux, once beaten by the plague in Oran, were to begin spreading it to
other towns himself.

On this level the story is undoubtedly feeble, but it has more interest
if viewed in the light of other works by Camus. In several places it
reminds us of these. The expression 'the water of night' is used also at
the end of the preceding story in the collection entitled 'The
Adulterous Woman', where its clear erotic connotation leaves little
doubt about a similar tone in this context:

> Her whole belly pressed against the parapet as she strained towards
> the moving sky; she was merely waiting for her fluttering heart to

calm down and establish silence within her. The last stars of the constellation dropped their clusters a little lower on the desert horizon and became still. Then, with unbearable gentleness, the water of night began to fill Janine, drowned the cold, rose gradually from the hidden core of her being and overflowed in wave after wave, rising up even to her mouth full of moans. The next moment, the whole sky stretched out over her, fallen on her back on the cold earth.

Exile and the Kingdom, Penguin ed., p. 29

Nor does the last sentence of 'The Renegade' ('a handful of salt fills the mouth of the garrulous slave') fail to remind us of 'Open the gates, let the wind and salt come and scour this town' at the end of Camus's play *State of Siege.* Most significant of all, we remember twice in 'The Renegade', the crucial moments in *The Outsider* before Meursault kills the Arab: 'my eyes corroded by the swords of salt and fire' echoes 'the keen blade of light flashing up from the knife, scarring my eyelashes, and gouging my eyeballs'; and 'I can't endure this endless heat, this waiting, I must kill him' could almost have been uttered by Meursault himself at the moment he fires on the Arab. These parallels show that 'The Renegade' is not an isolated phenomenon in the Camusian *oeuvre,* but a text that we would expect to betray preoccupations which underlie, if less explicitly, the major works also, so that a psychoanalytical interpretation of this story should suggest kindred exegeses elsewhere, particularly in *The Outsider.*

'The Renegade' opens on quotation marks; only the very last line (quoted above) lies outside the renegade's monologue. Thus it is not easy to be sure whether all the events in the story actually 'happened': the hero could hardly be described as 'garrulous' with his tongue cut out, and yet we are evidently invited to take as solid bedrock this description at the end, uttered by an independent, anonymous narrator (the familiar kind of implied author, who also tells the story of Janine, the 'adulterous woman' of the preceding story). If his tongue really were cut out, the hero could not be expected to produce much more than an incoherent croak, like the *gra* which punctuates his monologue. Thus if we can assume that the later sections of his monologue are fantasy, it would be natural for him to keep up the pretence to himself by uttering 'gra', like a refrain.

All we are authorized to accept is that, as the anonymous narrator puts it, the man is a 'slave'. We can thus assume the 'truth' of the story up to the moment of his enslavement in the house of the fetish. It would therefore not be unreasonable to suppose that he *imagines* his mutilation, apparently in order to punish and humiliate himself for his apostasy. This is supported by the evidence of his masochism, as for example when he gloats on the punishments inflicted on a previous representative of the church:

> They had whipped him and driven him out into the desert after having put salt on his wounds and in his mouth, he had met nomads who for once were compassionate, a stroke of luck, and since then I had been dreaming about his tale, about the fire of the salt and the sky, about the House of the Fetish and his slaves, could anything be more barbarous, more exciting be imagined, yes, that was my mission and I had to go and reveal to them my Lord.

pp.32-33

This old priest had also had his mouth stuffed with salt, but since he was able to speak to the neophyte, it is clear that his tongue was not cut out: which would seem to corroborate the interpretation advanced just now of the renegade's mutilation as fantasy. The facts, therefore, would seem to be that the inhabitants of the city of salt quite naturally tortured with salt, but that their cruelty ended there.

Given a basic masochism in the renegade (a masochism reflected in his adoration of power and brute force), we can then ask why he feels the need to punish himself by imagining such a barbarous mutilation. The answer seems to lie in his hatred of his father and in his parricidal instincts (he keeps saying 'my coarse father', 'my pig of a father', 'kill one's father'), a hatred naturally giving rise to a dread of castration. It is only a step to actually imagining such a 'castration'. This is plainly shown not only in the mutilation scene but also in the occurrence of words like 'ankles tied' (read 'testicles' in this context), 'cut off the chaplain's you know what', 'sexless', 'sterile', 'belly', 'groove', 'slits', 'hole', 'mouth', 'possessed', 'enslaved': the hero clearly sees himself progressively to have been emasculated and womanized (even the 'gag' has menstrual connotations). Having been a spectator at a copulation, he is punished, i.e. punishes himself, in a manner made familiar by the researches of psychoanalysts into early childhood and the Oedipus complex.

One of Freud's most gifted disciples, Melanie Klein, wrote (in

Contributions to Psycho-Analysis) of one of her young neurotic patients:

> The castration complex was extraordinarily strong . . . Without
> doubt auditory observation of coitus at the age of five—through an
> open door—then probably visual observation of it as well between
> the ages of six and seven, when he shared his parents' bedroom for a
> short time, served to intensify all his difficulties . . . [His]
> observations of sexual intercourse were carried out in such a way
> that the principal interest was directed to the accompanying
> sounds.

Sounds, too, are primordial in the renegade's case: he hears, but is not
permitted to observe, the rape of the woman by the sorcerer. Like an
infant, he longs to imitate this act, in which the father-figure asserts his
rights over the desired mother-figure, and this naturally gives rise to
the urge to castrate the father and supplant him. But, like another of
Mrs Klein's patients, 'being afraid of what he unconsciously felt the
desire to do, he expected always the same things to be done to himself'.
This is precisely the pattern in 'The Renegade': observation of
intercourse prompts a wish to imitate it, leading to fear of retribution,
which causes the renegade to imagine a mutilation that clearly
symbolizes castration by the father-figure. The next stage can also be
explained in Mrs Klein's terms. One of her delinquent young patients,
'feeling overwhelmed and castrated, had to change the situation by
proving to himself that he could be the aggressor himself'. This is
exactly what the renegade does: having been brutally punished, he
turns into an aggressor himself, and murders his successor, or at least
imagines he does.

The implications for *The Outsider*, written over fifteen years before
'The Renegade', are interesting. Although the concept of the Oedipus
complex is primarily a working hypothesis which has given rise to
successes in clinical psychiatry, I think we can agree with Freud that:

> It is once again an interesting fact that the Oedipus complex, which
> has been rejected from real life, has been left to imaginative writing,
> has been placed freely, as it were, at its disposal. Otto Rank has
> shown . . . how the Oedipus complex has provided dramatic authors
> with a wealth of themes in endless modifications, softenings and
> disguises—in distortions, that is to say, of the kind which we are
> already familiar with as the work of a censorship.

Standard Ed., XV, p.208

One of Camus's ideals was that a literary work, while working on several levels, should be a 'disguised confession'; but at the same time he had a real sense of decency, a *pudeur* which reveals itself in his strictures (expressed in his review of the book) on Sartre's 'obscenity' in *Intimacy* . All of what other critics have seen in *The Outsider,* as well as Camus's own comments on the novel, of course stand, but I would maintain that we are justified in seeing another level of meaning which has not been sufficiently brought out.

It can be hardly be a coincidence that, as Camus put its, Meursault is executed 'because he didn't weep at his mother's funeral'; the notion of a condemnation for not manifesting enough concern for his mother is emphasized in several places. This is however to some extent another issue, one I discussed in Chapter 3: the occurrence in the novel of the words 'mother', 'mamma', 'nest', 'belly', 'breasts', 'father', 'child', and 'son' should also be seen in the light of the fundamental antagonism between the hero and the dominant father-figure, the sun. The conflict between these two elements is a struggle to the death: the fight is over the mother-figure, that is, ultimately, the earth and the sea. (The associations between sun and father, and between earth and mother, are of course traditional ones in anthropology).

The hostility of the sun to Meursault is continually emphasized: it strikes him physically 'like a clenched fist', makes his temples throb: its glare is 'dazzling', it is so 'crushing'; it nails him down, and its heat is almost unbearable. In the novel most references to heat tend in fact to crystallize round four main episodes: the funeral, the murder, the first interrogation and the trial. The funeral, the murder and the end of the novel, in particular, are centres of great linguistic activity where the tension of the subject-matter is reflected in the density and heightened imagery of the writing. It is the sun which provokes Meursault to fire on the Arab—as he ingenuously but truthfully tells the amused court—and it is not the Arab he is trying to destroy, but the sun glinting on the knife-blade, and seeming to gouge out his eyes. The reasons for the sun's supposed antagonism are not far to seek: it arose in reaction to Meursault's relationship with the earth-mother and especially her watery aspect, the sea (there may be a link here with the salty uterine fluid). Meursault's union with the sea is touched upon at least three times. The first occurs when soon after his mother's death he meets Marie in the water, and lays the foundation of his seduction of her later that day. The next morning, he says, 'I sniffed the smell of brine that Marie's head had left on the pillow'. On the next occasion,

Marie teaches him a game which consists of spouting sea-water out of one's mouth against the sky, and soon after they hurry back to his bed. The third time they repeat the game and embrace in the water: 'I felt her legs twining round mine, and my senses tingled', Meursault recalls. Once in prison, he can still look at the sea (that is, gaze on the mother-figure), but after his sentence (i.e. the infliction of the paternal punishment) his cell is changed and he is deprived of the view.

Furthermore the *crime passionnel* aspect of the murder of the Arab is underlined by at least three indications: Meursault gazes at the sea, then as the crisis approaches he remembers that 'small waves were lapping the hot sand in little flurried gasps', and at the final moment 'a fiery gust came from the sea'. The erotic content of these indications is striking: the sea presses her 'lover' on with her amorous attentions. The sensual links between Meursault and the earth are also hinted at in other passages, the most significant of which is that which immediately precedes the funeral: the mourners' feet sink into the road-tar 'leaving bare its shiny pulp', or, as the revealing manuscript variant reads, 'its black flesh'. Finally, it is of note that the sun, in causing the earth to 'quiver', makes her 'inhuman and discouraging', and that later on 'the light seemed to swell up against the window'. Meursault, jealous of the sun's possession, seeks to flee into the earth's bosom, longs for protective shadow, and welcomes the truce of evening, but all in vain: the sun extorts its revenge and he is tried when summer heat returns again But Meursault is unrepentant: in the death-cell, he declares, he still loves 'this earth'.

We can perhaps see here a clear parallel with the legend of Oedipus. Three hints emphasize it: the frequent reference to feet (Oedipus means 'swell-foot'; Jung has noted in *Symbols of Transformation* that 'the foot as the organ nearest the earth, represents in dreams the relation to earthly reality and often has a generative or phallic significance'); the detail from a story Meursault remembers about the Czech's mother hanging herself (like Jocasta, and also like the mother in Camus's play *Cross Purpose*); and the way Meursault's crime is deliberately confused by the prosecutor with that of the parricide whose trial is to follow his own. Thus Meursault finds himself in the situation of one of the most famous of tragic heroes: the stage is set for the unfolding of his own tragedy. This is marked by a classical feeling of inevitability. Meursault wonders, in the morgue, whether he should smoke, and reflects that it is of no importance what he decides; a little later, at the funeral, the nurse states that if you walk too slowly, you risk sunstroke, if too quickly, a chill—whereat Meursault comments, 'either way one was for it'. Then, shortly before the murder, he says: 'I thought . . . that one could either fire, or not fire . . . to stay, or make a move, it came to much the same . . . it struck me that all I had to do was to turn, walk away and think no more about it'. At the end of the novel, he speaks of 'a single fate "choosing" him', reminding us of Oreste's cry in Racine's tragedy *Andromaque:*

> Je me livre en aveugle au destin qui m'entraîne
> (I yield blindly to the fate that sweeps me along).

He refers also to the 'mechanism' in which he is caught, and wonders at the beginning of the last chapter 'if the inevitable admits to a loophole', but decides 'there is no chance at all, absolutely none'. This naturally calls to mind the famous definition of tragedy given by the chorus in Anouilh's *Antigone*, a play which, in a less subtle way, reflects issues close to those with which Camus is concerned throughout *The Outsider:*

> So there we are. The spring is now wound up. Now all it's got to do is unwind by itself. That's what's so neat about tragedy, a light touch and it starts, the least thing, a second's glance at a passing girl raising her arms in the street, an itch for honour on waking one fine morning, like the craving for a tasty morsel, or one question too many one evening . . . That's all. After that you can leave it alone. No need to worry. It works all by itself. It's cunningly built, and well oiled since the beginning of time. Death, treachery and despair are all there, ready, as are the explosions, the storms and the silences; every silence: the silence when at the end the executioner's hand is raised; the silence when the shouts of the crowd burst upon the victor's ears . . . In tragedy you've no cause for anxiety. In the first place, you're all in it together. You're innocent after all! There's no significance in the fact that one does the killing and another is killed. It's a question of casting. And then, tragedy is above all restful, because you know there's no longer any hope, cowardly hope, that you're caught, caught like a rat, with all heaven about your ears, and that all you can do is yell—not groan or complain—just bawl at the top of your voice what you've always wanted to say, what you've never said, what you may not even have known before.

The Outsider is such a tragedy, in the ancient mould: man against the gods. It is so even in form to some extent: the first chapter can be seen as a prologue, the last as an epilogue; the 'robot woman' may represent the sphinx of the Oedipus legend, and the old people in the morgue, followed later by the spectators and jury in the courtroom, are a kind of silent chorus. It is, however, a pagan tragedy, and moves in a sphere from which the Christian God is excluded; Meursault dies 'without hope' of any after-life, and without even much confidence in the ultimate justice of the natural order. But as in great tragedy, although he 'knows' that he is moving towards disaster, this knowledge cannot prevent the ineluctable functioning of the 'mechanism'. The famous 'raps on the door of my undoing' are the signal that the point of no return has been reached, but there have (as for Oedipus) been previous warnings. And once he has 'shattered the balance of the day' he is left 'defenceless' against the machinations of a vindictive destiny. As I argued in Chapter 3, Camus is firmly on his side in his defiance of that destiny; he would, I suspect, have felt little sympathy for Freud's rather prudish comment on Sophocles's *Oedipus Rex*: 'fundamentally it is an amoral work: it absolves men from moral responsibility, exhibits the gods as promoters of crime and shows the impotence of the moral impulses of men which struggle against crime'.

Camus, who pondered just as much as Freud did the example of the Greeks, dreamed of great modern tragedy and believed that the climate was propitious for its birth. In basing *The Outsider* on the Oedipus myth, he was able to give Meursault the stature of a tragic hero. When he returned to the same theme in 'The Renegade', his grip had inevitably slackened: the Oedipal motif is both more obvious and less artistically controlled. In *The Outsider*, however, this theme, being more discreet, underlies the novel, but does not swamp it. Owing to the fact that the sureness of his technique matched the force of his insight into the tragedy of contemporary man, he was able to achieve his ideal of a work in which realism was tempered by symbolism and which was able to 'give man the power of language in his battle with his destiny'. Never was he more justified in describing himself as 'a creator of myths on the scale of his passion and anguish' than in his first novel.

V

Similarly, it is obvious that a work as complex at Beckett's *Molloy* can be read on many levels. The most immediate level is that of the detective novel. Moran is a kind of private eye who shadows Molloy, but then loses his vocation, abandons his assignment and resigns his office. *Molloy* would thus take its place in the sort of fiction in which the sleuth or spy is a type of antihero in the style of *The Third Man* or *The Spy Who Came In From The Cold*, works characterized by a deliberate refusal of the romantic, of the prestige traditionally attaching to the classic detective or spy, such as Sherlock Holmes or James Bond.

Molloy can also be read, at least as far as certain passages are concerned, as a modern transposition of the Ulysses legend. Molloy's stay in the police station, for instance, is not without affinities with the *Odyssey* episode of the Cyclops, and the young woman who approaches him on the beach suggests Nausicaa. More striking is the return of Moran-Odysseus, who finds no Penelope, however, and slaughters no suitors (his servant Martha having already left and his bees having died), but he cleans the slate anyway ('all there was to sell I have sold') and can receive Jacques-Telemachus back again under the paternal roof. And we may certainly see in Edith a new Calypso and in Lousse the witch Circe, for she puts a drug in Molloy's beer and holds him, he believes, by spells; if she does not transform him into a pig, it is stated that he replaces the dead dog which 'she had loved like an only child'. If we look a little closer at the Lousse-Circe parallel, it will enable us to interpret the hidden meaning of this strange novel, the plot of which may be summarized in the following terms (page numbers refer to the Calder one-volume edition of the Trilogy).

At the beginning of the first part (pp. 7-8), Molloy tells us that he is in his mother's room, having been brought there 'perhaps in an ambulance, certainly a vehicle of some kind,' since it was 'last year' that he ceased to walk. Having taken his mother's place, he does not know what has become of her. He has now to write out his story for a man who comes to collect his pages once a week, and he describes, in a sort of vision, how his last journey began. He was on a hilltop, crouched in the shadow of a rock, from which he watched two men walk towards each other along a country road, meet, exchange a few words, and then go their separate ways; he calls them A and C (pp. 8-

15). The man C has a cocked hat which Moran describes, when he sees it later in the novel, as 'quite extraordinary, in shape and colour ... like none I had ever seen,' and he carries a stout stick which Molloy later calls a club, when he thinks of the man again at the edge of the forest; and it is with this club in hand that C approaches Moran in the woods. After this important preliminary apparition Molloy declares that on waking he determined to go and see his mother (pp. 15-20). 'I needed, before I could resolve to go and see that woman, reasons of an urgent nature,' and the reasons that now impel him are connected with the need to establish 'our relations on a less precarious footing'. He fastens his crutches (without which, having a stiff leg, he is unable to walk) to the crossbar of his bicycle and sets out. On reaching the ramparts of his town he is arrested and later questioned by a sergeant at the police station for some obscure irregularity in his manner of resting on the bicycle (pp. 20-26). Released only later that afternoon, he goes to the country and some time afterward finds himself back in the town (he is no longer sure it is his mother's town, pp. 26-32), where he runs over a dog, whose owner, a woman called Lousse, protects him from the indignation of the bystanders and gives him lodging in her own home (pp. 32-60). He in some way replaces the dead animal in her affections and stays a 'good while' with her, quite unable to leave, no doubt (he thinks) because she drugs his food. There he loses track of his bicycle, and eventually leaves without it, on crutches only, his initial concern to discover its whereabouts having changed to indifference. Molloy strongly hints that Lousse kept him for sexual reasons, but she makes no attempt to prevent his departure. After leaving her, he wanders around the town and contemplates settling in a blind alley; he even attempts unsuccessfully to commit suicide. Finally, leaving the town in some haste, he spends a while at the seaside, renewing the stock of sucking stones that keep him from feeling hungry. Soon, however, his mother's image begins again to harry him, and he moves inland through a forest, where his progress becomes slower and slower. A charcoal-burner, 'sick with solitude probably,' offers his unwanted affections to Molloy and is soundly belaboured for his pains. No longer able to hobble, Molloy next takes to crawling, hears a voice saying 'don't fret, Molloy, we're coming,' and finally sinks into the bottom of a ditch at the very edge of the forest (pp. 60-91). It is from this ditch, evidently, that he is rescued in order to write his story in his mother's room, although he does not know what has become of her. Part I is thus circular, because the end refers to the beginning and vice versa.

The speaker in the second part gives his name as Jacques Moran and shows himself to be a meticulous individual, a practising Catholic, a fairly affluent householder very proud of his property, and an employee of a mysterious agency (run by a man called Youdi) which has asked for the report we are to read (p. 92). Moran's story begins one Sunday in summer when he is disturbed by Gaber, an agency messenger, who gives him urgent instructions to leave at once with his son, also called Jacques Moran, and look for a man whose name, says Gaber, is Molloy, but which to Moran sounds more like Mollose. In any case, the individual in question is 'no stranger to' Moran, whose disquiet grows throughout the day: the affair, at first dismissed by Gaber as 'nonsense,' soon shows itself to be 'no ordinary one' and begins to make Moran 'anxious,' then 'confused,' until finally he admits that he is 'losing his head' and 'floundering, I so sly as a rule.' Having missed the last mass, he solicits private communion, which brings him no relief, and his lunch, eaten too late, lies heavily on his stomach. Painfully and laboriously, he prepares to set out (pp. 92-128). He feels for the first time a sharp pain in his knee, while he is giving an enema to his son.

We are informed that Moran's job requires that he track down certain individuals and then deal with them in accordance with particular instructions; sometimes he is asked for a report. In the case of Molloy, however, he is not sure what he should do with his quarry once he finds him, because he cannot remember what Gaber said on this point. He never finds out, for he has not been long on his journey (pp. 128-165) before the pain strikes his knee again, paralysing his leg. He sends his son to the nearest town to buy a bicycle so that they may proceed unhindered; the boy is away three days. During this period two important things happen to Moran. First, the man whom Molloy designated C, or someone very like him, approaches Moran in the woods and asks for a piece of bread. Complying with this request, Moran asks in return to be allowed to feel the weight of the man's stick, and the next day he breaks off a heavy stick like it for himself. He is poking his fire with this stick when a different man accosts him. This man, who bears a close resemblance to Moran himself, asks if the old man with the stick has passed by. Moran, 'trembling all over', replies in the negative and orders his alter ego out of the way, but to no effect; so he clubs the man to death. 'He no longer resembled me,' adds Moran with evident relief, and his stiff leg, for a short while at least, bends normally again. Now that the self has been subjugated, reconciliation is possible with the antiself.

When his son returns with the bicycle, Moran says nothing about these events, and eventually, with the son riding and the father on the carrier, they reach Molloy's region. After a violent quarrel one night, Jacques abandons his father, and soon after, Gaber appears with an order for Moran to return home. Moran does so (pp. 165-175), assailed by growing decrepitude; he finds his house deserted, his bees dead, and his hens running wild. He determines to write his report and then leave again, to try to become free, to reject his manhood, and to live close to the earth (pp. 175-6). Thus this second part, in which the report is mentioned both at the beginning and at the end, is also circular.

In Leopold von Sacher-Masoch's novel *Venus in Furs*, the hero Séverin speaks in these words of the legendary witch Circe:

> I am once again seated under the arbour and reading in the Odyssey the story of the charming sorceress who transformed her worshippers into savage beasts. A most delightful image of love among the Ancients.

The metaphysic of suffering in Sacher-Masoch can serve as Ariadne's thread in the exploration of this labyrinth. According to Gilles Deleuze's masterly exposition, Sacher-Masoch's system is based on the concept of a 'wrong done to the father'. It is in order that he may atone for this wrong, and at the same time avenge himself on the father for the guilt feelings the latter inspires, that Sacher-Masoch's hero goes through the following process:

> The masochist would seek to identify himself with the mother in order to offer himself to the father as a sexual object, but, encountering now the danger of castration which he had tried to avoid, he would choose 'to be beaten', both as a means of warding off castration and as a regressive substitute for 'being loved'; the mother would then take on the role of the beating agent through the repression of the homosexual choice. Or, alternatively, the masochist would cast the wrong on to the mother . . . and would turn this to advantage, either in order to identify himself with this bad mother under cover of the projection and attain thereby the possession of the penis (perversion-masochism), or on the contrary in order to thwart this identification, while preserving the

projection, and offer himself as the victim (moral masochism).[1]

These themes can be discerned clearly in *Molloy*. The father in Beckett's writings figures most often as one set up in judgment, or as a tyrant, or else as a maleficent deity: he may (to cite only a few names) be called Godot, or Mr Knott, or Youdi. In the radio play *Embers* Henry timorously addresses himself directly to the shade of his dead father:

> You would never live this side of the bay, you wanted the sun on the water for that evening bathe you took once too often. But when I got your money I moved across, as perhaps you may know. We never found your body, you know, that held up probate an unconscionable time, they said there was nothing to prove you hadn't run away from us all and alive and well under a false name in the Argentine for example, that grieved mother greatly. I'm like you in that, can't stay away from it, but I never go in, no, I think the last time I went in was with you.

Like all Beckett's texts, this densely-wrought passage calls for detailed exegesis. Here, as in Camus's *The Outsider*, the sea represents the mother whose person is denied firmly to the son. After the death of the father (whose body was never found, symbolizing the repression by the son of the paternal image), the son finds the courage to defy his interdicts and cross the bay, thereby indulging his incest-fantasy. But the son's temerity is a relative thing, for he still depends on the father; before he disappeared, the latter 'glared' at his offspring, calling him a 'washout', thus denying all valid connection between his wife and their son (Beckett's French translation, 'avorton', makes this quite clear).

The idea of a wrong committed against the father is one of the leading themes in *Molloy*. The narrator of the first part confesses at once that he is 'scolded' by 'this man who comes every week' if he has written nothing, and asserts, two pages further on, 'it's my fault', only to ask at once: 'Fault? . . . But what fault?' A little later, Molloy declares that C 'was innocent, greatly innocent' and adds, after some

---

[1] *Présentation de Sacher-Masoch, avec le texte intégral de la Vénus à la fourrure,* by Gilles Deleuze (Paris: Editions de Minuit, 1967), p. 92; abbreviated henceforth as 'Deleuze'. For the sake of convenience I translate the French not only of Gilles Deleuze's introduction but also of Aude Willm's careful rendering of the accompanying German novel, *Venus in Furs*. It hardly needs saying that throughout this section I use the terms 'masochist' and 'sadist' in their scientific senses and am in no way suggesting the existence of any so-called 'perversion' in the characters or anyone else.

reflection: 'What business has innocence here? What relation to the innumerable spirits of darkness? It's not clear'. It is not clear, in truth; it cannot be clear, for the memory of the crime for which he feels obscurely guilty has been repressed. The crime was that of wishing to usurp with the mother the position of the father. And yet the longing to take the father's place is quite overt. As I have said, Molloy's confession begins in these terms:

> I am in my mother's room. It's I who live there now. I don't know how I got there ... I sleep in her bed. I piss and shit in her pot. I have taken her place. I must resemble her more and more. All I need now is a son.

The father is so firmly excluded that the son imagines, in accordance with a typically masochistic progression, that he is the fruit not of sexual relations between the hated father and the adored mother (relations which take on the aspect of rape, in the child's eyes), but of parthenogenesis.

None of this of course relieves the son of 'anxiety', and the words 'fellow-convict' and 'justice' occur frequently under his pen. But he is incorrigible and wishes to cede nothing of his recently-assumed prerogatives:

> Shall I describe the room [his mother's]? No. I shall have occasion to do so later perhaps. When I seek refuge there, beat to the world, all shame drunk, my prick in my rectum, who knows.

p.19

But Molloy, the writer, has already taken up residence in his mother's room, as he explains at the beginning of his confession; he is concerned that events be recounted in the chronological order of their occurrence and so here uses a future tense, 'when I seek ...'. More significant is the vulgar detail, 'my prick in my rectum', which calls for two comments. First the expression reflects the circular nature of Molloy's confession which I drew attention to earlier. Second, the perspicacious reader does not fail to notice that the narrator denies the father, in symbolically robbing him of his virile member: since he cannot endow the mother with a penis, he obliges the father not only to appear as a woman but also to render his sexual organ inoperative. The paternal penis, placed in the manner Molloy describes, is thus reduced to autoeroticism and thereby rendered incapable of harming the sacred, quasi-virginal image of the mother. In this connection another passage is revealing: Molloy is grateful to his mother for having made a serious attempt to abort him (a truly masochistic theme of punishment inflicted by the woman), and adds: 'I also give her credit for not having done it again, thanks to me, or for having stopped in time, when she did' (p. 19). He thus pays homage to 'that poor old uniparous whore' for having fled his father's caresses and thereby guaranteed that he be 'the last of [his] foul brood'.

The narrator is so strongly attracted by the mother-figure that he sometimes confuses the three women of classic masochism to which Gilles Deleuze has drawn attention, the harlot-mother (Edith in Molloy's story), the sadist-mother (Lousse), and the ideal mother who stands between the two extremes (Mag, the 'true', uterine mother). In a key passage Molloy clarifies an idea which disturbs him, not without reason:

> And I am quite willing to go on thinking of her [Lousse] as an old woman, widowed and withered, and of Ruth [Edith] as another, for she too used to speak of her defunct husband and of his inability to satisfy her legitimate cravings. And there are days, like this evening, when my memory confuses them and I am tempted to think of them as one and the same old hag, flattened and crazed by life. And God forgive me, to tell you the horrible truth, my mother's image sometimes mingles with theirs, which is literally unendurable, like being crucified, I don't know why and I don't want to.
>
> p. 59

Why 'crucified' exactly? Because, as Gilles Deleuze has explained, 'the two great masculine characters in Masoch's work are Cain and Christ'; similarly in Beckett's writings. In both authors Cain and Jesus typify men who deserve praise for killing the representation of the father, Cain in assassinating his brother, Christ in destroying the incarnation of the father by dying on the cross in an ultimate act of masochistic self-immolation. For their courageous action both heroes suffered. This explains not only their appeal to Sacher-Masoch, but also these words of Molloy's: 'I have gone in fear all my life, in fear of blows' (punishment dreaded but also sought after), and Estragon's in *Waiting for Godot*: 'All my life I've compared myself to [Christ]' (end of Act I).

'The trebling of the mothers has literally expelled the father from the masochist universe ... The masochist contract excludes the father, and transfers to the mother the responsibility for enforcing and applying the paternal law' (Deleuze, pp. 56, 81). This is why Molloy speaks not only of 'settling this matter between my mother and me' but also of 'establishing our relations on a less precarious footing' (p. 87). The first phrase would seem to refer to Molloy's concern to elicit information about his farther, whose name he confesses to be ignorant of. The second indicates a contract analogous to those which Gilles Deleuze expounds. The quasi-juridical nature of this contract is indicated by Molloy himself:

> I would have had the feeling, if I had stayed in the forest, of going against an imperative, at least I had that impression . . . I knew my imperatives well, and yet I submitted to them. It had become a habit. It is true that they nearly all bore on the same question, that of my relations with my mother, and on the importance of bringing as soon as possible some light to bear on these and even on the kind of light that should be brought to bear and the most effective means of doing so.
>
> p.86

Like Sacher-Masoch's hero Molloy elects to serve the dominating mother in a world from which he makes every effort to exclude the father (on whose behalf 'this man' fetches the manuscript pages every Sunday). These efforts are vain, however, because the father triumphs in the end. It is no doubt a Pyrrhic victory, but it presents analogies with the flagellation inflicted on Séverin by the Greek in *Venus in Furs*: a conclusion which 'characteristically marks the aggressive and hallucinatory return of the father to a world which had symbolically anulled him' (Deleuze, pp. 57, 244). This tyrant-father nonetheless allows the son to settle in the mother's room after the suppression (of which Molloy knows nothing, he tells us) of the mother, and thus to satisfy, under the paternal aegis, 'a deep and doubtless unacknowledged need, the need to have a Ma, that is a mother' (p. 17). All has returned to normal: the paternal authority, though briefly challenged, remains unaffected.

The riddle of the second part of the novel, made up of Moran's report, is solved by the perception that Moran is a younger Molloy (his physical condition at the end of the story is exactly that of Molloy at the beginning) and that the Moran who finally decides to exile himself from the world of men resembles the tramp Molloy who has difficulties with the police. It then becomes virtually certain that the 'chambermaid' by whom Molloy thinks he may have had a son is the servant Martha. She is thus Moran's mother, but he is unaware of the fact; when he is sent to look for Molloy, of course, he sets out, like Telemachus, *in search of his father*. Like Dickens in *Bleak House* or *Great Expectations*, indeed, Beckett has planted all the clues necessary to establish the interrelationships between his characters; but unlike Dickens he does not bring out explicitly what these are.

The two parts thus complement each other in a particularly profound way. Molloy, who is the masochist-type, sets out in search of his mother; Moran, who is the sadist-type, goes to look for his father. Molloy strives to eradicate the paternal image, Moran the mother's (he is ungentle to his mother Martha, and he has no regrets at the death of his wife Ninette in giving birth to his son, typically named after himself). Molloy gloats over his heterosexual encounters, Moran on his onanism, for 'the sadist does not recoil from his ultimate aim, the effective cessation of all procreation; . . . sadism offers the active negation of the mother and the inflation of the father, the father above every law' (Deleuze, p.53). This makes clear the reasons for the father-cult which is a basic feature of the second part of the novel: this panel of the diptych is the sadistic counterpart of the masochism of the other, and the work as a whole is a profound study of the sado-masochistic syndrome which is so firmly rooted in our psyche.

The interpretation that Moran is unknowingly the son of Molloy and Martha (the M's significantly link them as members of the same family) is supported by a curious detail which Moran ingenuously reports:

> I carried this sudden cordiality so far as to shake [Martha] by the hand, which she hastily wiped, as soon as she grasped my intention, on her apron. When I had finished shaking it, that flabby red hand, I did not let it go. But I took one finger between the tips of mine, drew it towards me and gazed at it. And had I had any tears to shed I should have shed them then, in torrents, for hours. She must have wondered if I was not on the point of making an attempt on her virtue. I gave her back her hand, took the sandwiches and left her. Martha had been a long time in my service.

> p.121

Martha's alarm comes from the fact that she thinks her son is about to overstep the Oedipal interdict. We know that the Oedipus myth is one with which Beckett is very familiar: Bruce Morrissette has recorded that he was the first to recognize the legend of the incestuous parricide in the detective plot of Robbe-Grillet's *Les Gommes*, and in *Watt* we read of 'Watt's Davus complex (morbid dread of sphinxes)'.

The theory that Molloy and Moran are one and the same person (an interpretation put forward by some critics) is invalidated by the categorical way in which Moran establishes a clear distinction between his mother (Martha, in all probability), his son's mother (Ninette), and Molloy's mother (the woman whose room Molloy occupies, that is, Moran's grandmother). No one would deny that the two men resemble each other, or even that Moran in a sense becomes Molloy, but we are not justified in assuming that no distinction is made between them.

Nonetheless, the resemblances between father and son in *Molloy* are even closer than has been generally noticed. In the context of what I said earlier about Moran's sadism, it should be noted that as his story unfolds Moran gradually changes, and from a good citizen and practising Catholic turns into a sceptic in religion and a social renegade indifferent to bourgeois ideals. But the most significant change concerns his sadism, which attains its paroxysm in the murder of his *persona* in the woods. After this act (of a violence surpassing even Molloy's brutality to the charcoal-burner) Moran turns slowly into a masochist in so far as he sees himself 'being reborn of the woman alone, having a second birth' and becoming 'the Man . . . without sexual love, property, country, antagonisms or work' (Deleuze, p.87). Moran, it will be remembered, is ordered to take his son with him on his last mission; this is because of the importance of the psychological transformation he will undergo as a result of it. It is the voice common to both Molloy and Moran which gives birth to the new Moran, just as it had whispered 'don't fret Molloy, we're coming' at the forest's edge. Moran expresses his rebirth in these terms:

> I have been a man long enough, I shall not put up with it any more, I shall not try any more. I shall never light this lamp again. I am going to blow it out and go into the garden . . . I have spoken of a voice telling me things. I was getting to know it better now, to understand what it wanted. It did not use the words that Moran had been taught when he was little and that he in his turn had taught to his little one. So that at first I did not know what it wanted. But in the end I understood this language. I understood it, I understand it, all wrong perhaps. That is not what matters. It told me to write this report.

p.176

The impulsion to record their experiences is also common to both men; each needs to get things straight, to place them 'on a less precarious footing,' and the mere exposition of their problem helps to solve it. Significantly, Martha, Moran's probable mother, has disappeared from the scene. As for the 'voice', it no doubt represents the feminine aspect of the godhead (*la voix*, in French), the male facet of which is represented by Youdi (cf. Yahweh, the sender of Gaber, i.e. Gabriel, and also Latin *iudex*, judge). At the end of both parts of the novel these two forces remain in uneasy equilibrium: Molloy and Moran respond to the voice, but they also obey the orders of the male overlord.

We are to deduce from all this, I believe, that the image of the mother dominates this novel as fruitfully as it does Camus's *Outsider*. Both Moran and Molloy are happy to take up a uterine position, and Molloy's hat is of course a figure of the caul. Moran definitely repudiates the father-figure and is reborn of the mother alone; Molloy finds his mother and Moran finds Molloy in the sense that he is reconciled with himself. The brutalities, like whipping in Sacher-Masoch, must be seen as violent destruction of the old self, a punishment (hence the stress laid on guilt) which makes rebirth possible. Martha, one sort of mother-figure, has disappeared in favour of a different mother-figure, the voice.

'How is it', Lévi-Strauss asks, 'that we do not have only one procreator, but a mother *plus* a father?' Life might well be simpler if we did; but the fact is, as Erich Fromm has shown, that one of the deepest longings in everybody is to keep the tie to mother. It is this aspiration which gives *Molloy* its profoundly disturbing quality and makes of this great novel its author's masterpiece, a work of satisfying unity in that a sadist-type, sent in search of a masochist-type, is imperceptibly transformed into the type sought. The circularity of the work thus lies deeper than in form alone. It is the circularity of psychological tensions resolved; as such it brings comfort. *Molloy*, like *Wuthering Heights* or *The Outsider,* is a novel not of mental sickness, but of an arduously won, and therefore doubly precious, breakthrough into a triumphant sanity.

CHAPTER SIX

The
Imprisoned Flame

CHAPTER SIX

The Imprisoned Flame

Quand sera brisé l'infini servage de la femme,
quand elle vivra pour elle et par elle,
l'homme, —jusqu'ici abominable, —lui ayant
donné son renvoi, elle sera poète, elle aussi! La
femme trouvera de l'inconnu! Ses mondes d'idées
différeront-ils des nôtres?—Elle trouvera des
choses étranges, insondables, repoussantes,
délicieuses: nous les prendrons, nous les
comprendrons.

RIMBAUD

I

'Don't make patterns out of coincidences', writes Kingsley Amis in *The Anti-Death League*: 'All pattern-making is bad.' In spite of this wise advice the critic cannot help making patterns out of what he reads: that is his job. A work of art demands not only to be interpreted intrinsically but also to be situated extrinsically: to be read for itself *and* placed within a cultural tradition. The patterns (within and without) which the critic discerns will not correspond exactly to the patterns which other readers discover for themselves: but in the continual debate about art some generally-agreed shape is seen to emerge. In *The Great Tradition* F.R. Leavis argues that the main current in fiction in English ran through Jane Austen, George Eliot, Henry James and Joseph Conrad, novelists one thinks of as being distinguished above all by critical intelligence. But there is another tradition in the English-language novel: it runs from Emily Brontë through Melville to Patrick White, Malcolm Lowry and Wilson Harris, and is an imaginative, even visionary mode. If Leavis's 'great tradition' is closest to the central current of the French novel in which the most interesting issue is the formal one, the other mode brings English writing more into harmony with some of the greatest

123

existential novels, with Dostoyevsky's *Crime and Punishment* or with Céline's *Journey to the End of the Night*. It is with this more 'visionary' mode—especially as it relates to writing by and about women—that the present chapter deals.

II

For man has not always used literature to understand the world and his place in it through acts of critical intelligence. The novel, as we can see in the course of this book, has been employed to probe not only the personal and cultural relationships which form the basis of our social codes, but also the hidden, secret recesses of the human psyche, the areas held under the strongest taboos. Foremost among these—providing a powerful impulse to fiction-making—is the erotic.

Eroticism is not the same thing as pornography, although the two are closely related. They both aim to arouse sexual emotions and reactions in the reader: but the difference between them lies in the fact that pornography is not concerned to achieve anything beyond arousal, whereas eroticism implies a whole view of the world, one in which man renders himself culpable of transgressing a taboo. A sense of guilt, a burning and exquisite feeling of shame lies at the heart of eroticism: such is the contention of the leading theorist of the subject, Georges Bataille, who argues in his book *Eroticism* (first published in 1957) that 'the alternating play of transgression and taboo is seen most clearly in eroticism'. Bataille views man as having evolved from primitive animality, from what he calls 'shame-free sexuality', to a condition in which on becoming aware of his mortality he has slid into 'shameful sexuality': and this has led directly to the development of eroticism. This explains, Bataille argues, why sex and death—the *eros* and *thanatos* of the Greeks—are so intimately linked in the human psyche that the orgasm is thought of as a 'little death', a moment out of time, a crisis of perfect loneliness and isolation. It also explains why mystics like Saint Teresa of Avila have expressed the violence of their religious emotions in terms of the ecstasy of the 'little death', and why violation and rapture are linguistically and conceptually such closely connected notions. Bataille's version of eroticism thus covers the awareness of, and fascination with, the idea of committing a fault, the notion of violation in the sense of forcing a shame, and nostalgia for what he terms 'the lost continuity': in eroticism we seek what, as discontinuous beings, we can never possess, the ideal of permanence and continuity. In the act of sex, he claims, we seize upon the illusion of timelessness and stability, so that eroticism is in his eyes 'the approbation of life even unto death. Sexuality is the raging storm by which we simultaneously fear and yearn to be swept away: hence the fact, which he expresses in one of his most illuminating paradoxes, that 'human life is unable without cheating to follow the movement which leads it towards death'. Hence, too, the notion of play which is as inseparable from eroticism as the notion of guilt, and the fact that the spasmic crisis of the sexual act is at one and the same time 'the most intense and the most insignificant' of all those we ever experience.

Bataille's paradox of the inextricable tragedy and frivolity of sexual love is one of the most profound and fruitful of all approaches to the erotic in life and art. Others seem either too earnest or too shallow, concerned for the most part with side issues like the relative nature of the obscene, the controversy over censorship, and so-called sexual liberation. But if Bataille enables us to understand most works in the western tradition of erotic characteristics, it is doubtful if he is of much assistance in understanding erotica written outside the Christian ethos. There seems little point, for instance, in evoking the notion of guilt in a reading of the Hindu classic on the art of love, the *Kama Sutra*. This is both a religious tract and a practical handbook; whereas the first aspect is inconceivable in the Christian canon, the second is the ancestor of the innumerable manuals on sex-technique which have proliferated in recent years. Bataille's definition is not of much help either in considering the erotic significance of the *Song of Songs*, that fragmentary wedding drama which has, somewhat incongruously, found its way into the Old Testament and is the subject in Christian exegetics of an elaborate allegorical interpretation which identifies the bridegroom as Christ and the bride as the Church. It has in reality much more to do with the epithalamia of Greece and Rome, the nuptial songs sung before the bridal chamber to celebrate in anticipation the legitimate joys of the married state. The imagery of the *Song of Songs* has, it is true, something in common with such twentieth-century poetry as André Breton's paean to the body of the loved one, *Union Libre*. The closing lines of this poem—

Ma femme aux yeux de savane
Ma femme aux yeux d'eau pour boire en prison
Ma femme aux yeux de bois toujours sous la hache
Aux yeux de niveau d'eau de niveau d'air de terre et de feu

—can, *mutatis mutandis*, be compared with King Solomon's words of amorous adulation in the Bible passage:

> How beautiful are thy feet in sandals, O prince's daughter!
> The joints of thy thighs are like jewels,
> The work of the hands of a cunning workman.
> Thy navel is like a round goblet,
> Wherein no mingled wine is wanting:
> Thy belly is like a heap of wheat
> Set about with lilies.

But similar as the imagery sounds, Breton's poem comes at the end of a long evolution which, in a manner, links up again across two millennia with pre-Christian attitudes to sexuality, in which uninhibited hedonism praised the beauty of the body and celebrated the joys of its possession. Breton's imagery, for all that, is more sophisticated and abstract, the result of a conscious act of liberation rather than a work composed in innocent awareness.

For what Christianity did to sexuality—as a result, among other documents, of the Epistles of Paul and the *Confessions* of Augustine—was to rob it, for at least eighteen centuries, precisely of its innocence. The poetry of the Troubadours and Dante's poignant lines on Paolo and Francesca (for example) are deeply marked by an awareness of transgression:

> Amor, che a nullo amato amar perdona,
>   mi prese del costui piacer sì forte,
>   che, come vedi, ancor non m'abbandona.
> Amor condusse noi ad una morta . . .

Inferno
V, 103-6

Or, to paraphrase Francesca's words, 'love, which spares no one, drove us to our death and even now haunts us in Hell'. Such notions would have sounded very strange to the authors of the *Kama Sutra* and the *Song of Songs*. Equally strange would have sounded Phèdre's accents early on in Racine's tragedy of 1677, when she utters the wish that her heart were as 'innocent' as her hands still happily are:

> Grâces au ciel, mes mains ne sont point criminelles.
> Plût aux Dieux que mon coeur fût innocent comme elles!

The power of eroticism, which leads Phèdre willy-nilly to destruction, is an object of obsessive fear also in many of the classics of the European novel, such as *Dangerous Liaisons*, or *Anna Karenina* (to which Tolstoy appended the stern epigraph 'Vengeance is mine, and I will repay'). Women, as in *Effi Briest*, or men, as in *Adolphe*, see their lives ruined by a sexual lapse; and the novelists who imagined these situations insisted on the universality of the application. His Emma, Flaubert was fond of repeating, wept in countless villages throughout France. 'Passion', Georges Bataille comments, 'involves us in suffering, since it is at bottom a quest for the impossible'. This observation sums up many 'sentimental educations' written both before and after Flaubert's, and one in particular: Prévost's *Manon Lescaut*, a minor novel of the early eighteenth century which has known many stage, operatic and screen adaptations as testimony to its archetypal quality and to the way it speaks to succeeding generations of the danger and the thrill of illicit love. 'No one would deny', writes Bataille, 'that an essential element in sexual excitation is the feeling of losing grip, of keeling over'. This sensation lies at the heart of the story told so pathetically to the Man of Quality by the Chevalier des Grieux. His amoral mistress, Manon, is characteristic of the teasing enigmatic courtesan who runs through European literature from *Fanny Hill* and *The Lady of the Camellias* to *The Woman of Rome*. There is no doubt about the abiding interest of the archetype: Manon's 'instinctive duplicity' recurs in many guises, not least in Proust's Albertine.

'It's the story of a knave and a whore' was Montesquieu's bluff verdict on this novel in which a young man of good family risks everything (including that worst of all fates for a gentleman, dishonour as a card-sharper) to follow a girl who loves him but cannot live without a plentiful supply of money, even if that necessitates being unfaithful to him to get it. When she is eventually transported to America as a prostitute he follows her, and as he is able to pass himself off for a time as her husband they live happily together in the New World, but Manon's beauty tempts the governor's son: when it is discovered that the pair are not married, Manon is claimed by the other man. She dies after the lovers escape together into the wilderness. The hero returns chastened to France, where he tells his story to the Man of Quality who has taken pity on him, succoured him, and of whose memoirs this tale purports to be a part. The book is thus a 'frame-novel', typical of its time. It has however been called 'one of the most immoral books in French literature'. This may at first appear an over-reaction in the case of such a sentimental tale, but we know that the Marquis de Sade thought highly of it and claimed that had it not been for Manon there would never have been his Justine, because Prévost showed that a 'fallen woman' could still be an object of pity and even of admiration. And Leopold von Sacher-Masoch mentions the novel twice in *Venus in Furs*, the hero of which comments, on the subject of the Chevalier, that love knows no virtue or merit, it simply adores, forgets and forgives.

So, clearly, this novel inspired much that was to come in erotic writing. That is quite understandable, since *Manon Lescaut* is ambivalent about good, evil, sanctity and transgression. The worthy Tiberge, the Chevalier's friend, is presented in the novel as a pillar of Christian chastity and honour, as Des Grieux's conscience in the dialogue which the book conducts between good and evil, but it is also suggested, rather slyly, that he is a prig. He appears to be immune to the power of the sexual instinct, an instinct whose disruptive potential the novel portrays realistically; or is he merely, to use a later terminology, strongly repressed? The eighteenth-century rhetoric and delicacy of expression do not conceal the fact that the relationship between the hero and the heroine is intensely and obsessively erotic: Manon admitted, Des Grieux tells us, that he was the only man who, as he discreetly puts it, 'could enable her to taste to perfection the sweet charms of love'. This strong physical involvement upsets the stability of the protagonists' lives, and when it is over, Des Grieux seems like a man emerging from a long addiction to some debilitating drug; but while under the influence he is shrewd in defence of his 'unreason'.

He does this by turning the traditional Christian argument about sex on its head. Instead of asserting that it is worth putting up with temporary pain in return for eternal bliss, Des Grieux lucidly argues that it is worth tolerating great future torment in return for transient but intense bliss. We are here at the heart of what Bataille has described in *Eroticism* as the deluded but persistent quest for transcendence through the sexual act. Thus the overt moral of the novel, that the sexual appetite is destructive and that predestination is remorseless, is subordinated to the subliminal moral, that the longing for an impossible, permanent ecstasy is a magnificent thing; and it is this second message which has spread so far and made the story so universally popular. It has all the ingredients needed for success: a story of blind, hopeless possession by love at first sight, a phenomenon of which we are all secretly afraid and yet charmed. Later discussions of the possibility—such as D.H. Lawrence's powerful stories of instinctive sexual communication between man and woman, from 'Second Best' to *Lady Chatterley's Lover*—are written in the shadow of the same archetype.

It is significant that one of the most erotic incidents in the history of motion pictures occurs in Ingmar Bergman's film *Persona* when the nurse describes to her patient what took place between her and a boy on a beach. In this entirely *verbal* description the image never moves out of the sick room; if the beach, and even the naked lovers, had been shown, the effect would have been less strong. Verbal descriptions of the sexual act, especially where (as in this example, or to take another, the copulation of Sarah and Charles in *The French Lieutenant's Woman* by John Fowles) there is a marked suggestion of the extraordinary, the prohibited, the clandestine or the unexpected, are often more suggestive than visual showings; as Bergman, unconsciously echoing Bataille, put it in an interview. 'the actress makes the scene so remarkable because she tells the story in a voice which carries a tone of shameful lust'. One cannot, after all, 'make' eroticism in the way one 'makes' love, but only think, say or write it; the erotic occurs not in the sphere of action, but of language and symbol. Prévost shows that he understood this perfectly well and made of *Manon Lescaut*, otherwise a rather unsatisfactory psychological novel, one of the classics of European erotic writing.

It came at the right time. Early novel writers tried to come to terms with eros bawdily, like Rabelais, Cervantes and Grimmelshausen, or solemnly, like Rousseau and Sade, or wittily like Marivaux and Fielding. The nineteenth-century novel was either wary of the subject, or dealt with it massively and sententiously (like Zola). Since the Decadents—among them Aubrey Beardsley, author of *The Story of Venus and Tannhäuser*—eroticism has emerged from under-the-counter pornography and gentlemen's smoking-room jests and begun to take its place as an integral element in art, with the novels of writers like Pauline Réage (whose *Story of O* is as we shall see a classic of female erotica), André Pieyre de Mandiargues (for whom 'the sex of woman is everywhere present, but like an armed trap, if not an open tomb') or Jean Genet (who has explored the anguish of eroticism at the homosexual level). Most of today's fiction contains a distinct and overt erotic element: 'eroticism', it has been said with some justice, 'is no longer defined by its secrecy'.

Literature can thus be used as a form of indirect confession: it has been the timid voluptuary's path to orgiastic indulgence, the would-be parricide's to slough off father, the potential voyeur's to fulfil his fantasies while remaining a respectable citizen. Most writers, in fact, work out fears, phobias or fantasies to a greater or lesser extent; the most interesting are not so much those who, like Sade, Genet or Sacher-Masoch, do so fairly consciously (even conscientiously), but those who may be only half-aware, if aware at all, of what they are doing. The critic eavesdrops on these, listens to the ambiguous confession, bringing together different texts, and contexts, and attempts to interpret it for the reader. In humility he transcribes a dialogue (the conversation which every writer holds with himself) in his attempt to bring some order into the divine chaos of the world he investigates. In the act of composing the dialogue the artist inevitably, and rightly, shuffles the cards and confuses the issues, and waits to be understood by what Stendhal called the 'happy few'. If in his sorting out of these ambiguities and evasions the critic joins the ranks of the few, he is doing his job fairly and well; he will have made a pattern and aided our understanding. I hope to do this in the next section, which deals with a few women novelists who explore the paradoxes of sexual love—especially as seen from the woman's point of view—which I have touched on here.

III

Only a year after the first performance of Racine's *Phèdre,* in 1678, Madame de La Fayette published *The Princess of Cleves* and with one stroke freed the novel of its association with romances and tales, and set it on its path as an art-form in its own right. It was not her only novel, but the others are negligible in comparison. It told the story of a woman who fell in love with a man who was not her husband, who refused to succumb to her passion, and even when her husband's death freed her to make an honourable love-match, remained single rather than risk the possibility that the man she loved would, having once possessed her, set off as he had so often in the past, in search of 'fresh woods, and pastures new'.

It is a novel, in other words, which sets the fine disorder of passion aside in favour of the joyless order of *ataraxia*, tranquility of mind, that quality so prized in the seventeenth century. Descartes advised his reader that one should take one's distance from one's passions to allow them to cool, then attack them, and win; had Madame de La Fayette been less of an artist, her book would in fact have read like a fictionalized version of such contemporary *idées reçues* in philosophy. Madame de Clèves, who likes her ideas 'clear and distinct', examines the reasons that oblige her to refuse Monsieur de Nemours, the man she loves, and finds them very strong, and so lets them govern her conduct, although his image is not 'erased' entirely from her heart. There are other conventional elements: Monsieur de Nemours 'happens' to be eavesdropping when Madame de Clèves is confessing her (innocent) love to her husband, and 'happens' to spy on her when, thinking she is unobserved, she gazes lovingly on his portrait. And Monsieur de Clèves's deathbed rhetoric does not move the modern reader as it no doubt did Madame de La Fayette's contemporaries.

But these are small things compared with the conquest of a new fictional manner that Madame de La Fayette carried out single-handed. She did not, like her predecessors, set her novel in Arcadia, but in sixteenth-century France, and her characters were not shepherds and shepherdesses, but the sort of people with whom she spent her life—courtiers and princes. Above all, the emotions were much nearer those of everyday life than any that had been portrayed before. The atmosphere of jealousy and sexual frustration is very different from the feelings imputed to the conventional swain sighing at cruel Phyllis's feet, and instead of stringing fairly incredible events together with no attempt at psychological plausibility, as her contemporaries did, Madame de La Fayette makes her plot develop rationally and inevitably, like a soundly-built tragedy.

The sedate (factual but rather precious) language of the opening pages sets the tone: the spotlight travels round the characters frozen in attitudes like wax figures, then picks out Monsieur de Clèves, followed by Monsieur de Nemours, the male protagonists in the triangular drama. In this royal court, the outside world does not obtrude at all: we are in an aristocratic milieu, metropolitan, non-provincial; space has yet to be conquered by the novel. Then the spotlight falls on Mademoiselle de Chartres, who is to become the Princess of Cleves: 'a beauty appeared at court, who attracted everybody's attention'. Then follows, imputed to the girl's mother Madame de Chartres, the statement which is the basis of this story, in that it dwells on the strength of passion and the need both for external self-defence and internal self-control:

Most mothers imagine that it is sufficient never to speak of illicit love in the presence of young persons in order to deflect them from it. Madame de Chartres was of the contrary opinion. She often described passion to her daughter. She showed her the pleasures it offered in order the more effectively to put the girl on her guard against its dangers. She told her all about how insincere, deceitful and unfaithful men could be, and to what domestic misery illicit affairs can lead. She pointed out to her on the other hand how tranquil the life of an honest woman was, and how much extra brilliance a well-born and attractive girl acquired from being chaste. But she stressed how hard it was for women to remain virtuous; it could only be achieved, she said, if they kept themselves severely under control and took good care to hold fast to what alone could make them happy, shared love within wedlock.

As in *Phèdre*, the sexual urge is seen as brutal, and infatuation, when it occurs, is both immediate and enduring: Monsier de Clèves falls in love with the girl at first sight, as she and Monsieur de Nemours later do with each other. As in Racine, again, sex is found in conjuction with another strong passion, ambition: it is a weapon in the power struggle at court. Madame de Chartres, having married her daughter to Monsieur de Clèves, sees her unknowingly fall in love with the newly-arrived Monsieur de Nemours, and he with her; she tries to warn her daughter, on her deathbed, of the perils she faces: 'you are in danger,' she says, 'of falling like other women'.

But Madame de Clèves is innocent of heart and so takes a long time to realize that she is in love with a man who is not her husband. Events force her, like Madame de Rênal, into self-awareness through pity and jealousy: pity for the loved one momentarily in danger, and jealousy over a letter from another woman which she imagines he has received. It is the pangs of jealousy which convince her, like Madame de Rênal, that she is deeply in love, just as later it is they which prompt her to relinquish all hope of marrying Nemours. But for the moment she is swept along by her feelings. The stress throughout, as in *Phèdre*, is on the impotence of the protagonists to dominate and control these. Tragedy, in fact, involves all the main characters and puts them on an equal footing; at the same time, the heroine does not suffer from false modesty, but like Racine's Hermione insists on her uniqueness: it is therefore doubly galling for her to find how similar she is to other women. Like Phèdre, too, she feels horror at herself after her husband's death of a broken heart, for which she takes the blame. Her sense of duty to his memory combines with her fear of Nemours's basic inconstancy to make her resolve not to marry him: 'passion may lead me', she declares with a fine defiance, 'but it cannot make me blind'. She does not give in, and the ensuing detachment, in time, enables her to overcome her love. Retreat is ultimately the only solution to the tragic dilemma: a retreat into oneself.

It seems at first as if the only way out of the claustrophobic atmosphere of the trap in which the heroine finds herself is to confess her innocent passion to her husband, but far from solving the problem, this merely provokes the tragic outcome. Here, as in Racine, the *dénouement* is a function as much of the temperament of the protagonists as of the situation in which they find themselves: it is the clash of character, rather than fate's decrees, which provokes disaster. But the end is perhaps more Cornelian than Racinian. 'Corneille's characters', writes Geoffrey Brereton, 'arrive by rational debate ... at a decision—it may be to sacrifice their lives. Racine's characters have no decision to take. Their world and they themselves have disintegrated.' Madame de Clèves is very unhappy, but she has not, by the end, disintegrated. She has dominated her destiny through strength of will; the odds were against her, but out of courage she has won. This is tragedy at its most invigorating: we are not necessarily 'as flies to wanton boys'; we can avoid becoming sport to the gods. Thinking mainly of this novel, Albert Camus said:

> Much of the genius of French fiction resides in this clear-sighted effort to set the cries of passion within the order of pure language. It is one of the secrets of the French novel that it can reveal at one and the same time a harmonious sense of fatality and an art arising directly from the freedom of the individual: that it can provide the ideal arena in which the forces of destiny come into head-on collision with human choice.

The Princess of Cleves stands at the point where man's fate and his freedom meet in face to face antagonism, and dispassionately, stubbornly (as Camus would add), sees the drama out. The fact that this clash was so perceptively documented by a woman writer gives it added poignancy. If one reads a lot of novels written by women it is difficult to avoid the feeling that they have a family air about them. It is partly that women appear, as G.H. Lewes noted as early as 1852, to write on the whole more immediately from their private experience than men; it is possible to discern in the painful odyssey followed by Edna O'Brien's narrator-heroines, for instance, Miss O'Brien's own journey from restricted Catholic girlhood in Ireland to the life of an emancipated freelance writer in London. Similarly, Iris Murdoch's interest in Paris and in French philosophy emerges obliquely from her first novel, *Under the Net*, even though she chooses to speak through a male narrator. And Margaret Drabble, married at the time to an actor, and mother of three children, does not stand far behind the heroines of her early novels who find themselves in much the same circumstances: we are not deceived when the university one of them went to is changed to Oxford, whereas Miss Drabble herself is a Cambridge graduate.

Of course there *are* women novelists who are just as interested as men in structural experiment, in developing the form of the novel: Madame de La Fayette, George Eliot, Virginia Woolf and Nathalie Sarraute are all names of considerable importance in the history of the genre. But in this they do not compete on equal terms with men. Madame de La Fayette was not a Cervantes, nor George Eliot a Tolstoy, nor Virginia Woolf a James Joyce; and Nathalie Sarraute is no Claude Simon, nor Hélène Cixous a Jorge Luis Borges. Women have been very great novelists indeed—Jane Austen and George Eliot in particular—but their greatness has been exercised, for obvious sociological reasons, on a narrower compass. It was George Eliot who first pointed out how frustrating it is 'to have a man's force of genius in you, and yet to suffer the slavery of being a girl', to undergo the ordeal of experiencing 'spiritual grandeur ill-matched with the meanness of opportunity'; how uncharacteristic, in this respect, was Cranford, which Mrs Gaskell describes as being a town 'in possession of the Amazons; all the holders of houses, above a certain rent, are women'. In creating the character of Gwendolen Harleth, George Eliot produced her *chef d'oeuvre*; but on Daniel Deronda, and generally in the 'Jewish' part of the novel, she wrote with a feebleness Tolstoy would not have been guilty of. He could combine the microcosm and the macrocosm in *War and Peace* and so could Stendhal in *The Charterhouse of Parma*. But, as Virginia Woolf says in *A Room of One's Own*, while George Eliot lived secluded in St John's Wood as the mistress of a married man, Tolstoy, on the other side of Europe, was 'living freely with this gypsy or with that great lady; going to the wars; picking up unhindered and uncensored all that varied experience of human life which served him so splendidly later when he came to write his books . . . Had Tolstoy lived at the Priory', Mrs Woolf goes on, 'he could scarcely . . . have written *War and Peace*'.

Compelled (at least until recently) by the restrictions of their biological and social condition to limit their focus, women have tended naturally to use fiction as a means of defining themselves, usually through a heroine surrogate; as Lewes perceived, they seek to assuage 'the sorrow that in silence wastes their lives'. Women novelists concentrate their attention on their heroine 'in all her independent physical and psychological reality' (Victor Dupont had argued) so that 'women's novels gain in depth what they lose in breadth and energy'. It also means, Dupont notes, that they betray 'a certain revolt against the oppression and stupidity of a world created by men in which women find themselves forced to live, and against the roles and functions which are assigned to them by men'.

In this act of self-definition and self-assertion, women writers have, not unnaturally, returned again and again to the image of the cage. Margaret Drabble's first novel, *A Summer Bird-Cage*, takes its title from John Webster's words, quoted at the head of the work: "'Tis just like a summer bird-cage in a garden: the birds that are without, despair to get in, and the birds that are within, despair and are in a consumption for fear they shall never get out'; women are seen as unable to leave the cage, even when the door is opened. This situation provokes writers about women's liberation to understandable anger: 'Five years ago', Germaine Greer noted in 1970 in *The Female Eunuch*, 'it seemed clear that emancipation had failed . . . the cage door had been opened but the canary had refused to fly out. The conclusion was that the cage door ought never to have been opened because canaries are made for captivity; the suggestion of an alternative had only confused and saddened them.' Miss Greer saw with despondency that 'the fear of freedom is strong in us', but her message, which comes over loud and clear—even a trifle stridently—is that if liberty is terrifying, 'it is also exhilarating'. Whatever the truth in this matter—that is, whether for their own ends women connive in their own enslavement, as Pauline Réage suggests in her erotic fantasy *Story of O*, or whether they have it cynically imposed on them by 'the psychological sell' as Germaine Greer believes—the nature of their imprisonment is carefully explored by their novelists, that is, by those who suffer and dream on their behalf. This is how Jane Eyre describes the surroundings of Thornfield, Mr Rochester's mansion to which she has come after spending a placid, uneventful, unexciting and lonely girlhood at Lowood school:

> Farther off were hills: not so lofty as those around Lowood, nor so craggy, nor so like barriers of separation from the living world; but

yet quiet and lonely hills enough, and seeming to embrace
Thornfield with a seclusion I had not expected to find.

Jane Eyre, Penguin ed., p. 101

Later, Jane climbs to the top of the house and gazes at the skyline,
longing to 'overpass that limit' and leap into a world where things
happen and where one meets a variety of different people. She
recognizes that many of her Victorian readers will blame her for being
'discontented', but she says she cannot help it. We feel for her when
she confesses that the restlessness of her nature 'agitated [her] to pain
sometimes' and forced her to seek solace in the world of her
imagination, 'quickened with all of incident, life, fire, feeling, that I
desired and had not in my actual existence'. This is sad; and sadder still
is the programme she sets out, reasonable enough in all
conscience—Charlotte was no radical, and was scathing about John
Stuart Mill's militancy on behalf of women's rights. What Jane Eyre
modestly asks for is that women should have 'exercise for their
faculties, and a field for their efforts as much as their brothers do; they
suffer from too rigid a restraint', she goes on, 'too absolute a
stagnation, precisely as men would suffer; and it is narrow-minded in
their more privileged fellow-creatures to say that they ought to confine
themselves to making puddings and knitting stockings, to playing on
the piano and embroidering bags' (pp. 110-111).

But things are not quite so simple as Jane makes out; she herself
reveals some of the paradoxes inherent in the issue of women's
liberation. She is dimly aware, for instance, that the key to
emancipation is sexual, or at least that the sexual threshold must first
be crossed before anything else can follow. She does not of course say
this outright, but her choice of imagery makes it clear enough:

> I went to my window, opened it, and looked out . . . My eye passed
> all other objects to rest on those most remote, the blue peaks. It was
> those I longed to surmount; all within their boundary of rock and
> heath seemed prison-ground, exile limits. *I traced the white road
> winding round the base of one mountain, and vanishing in a gorge
> between two.* How I longed to follow it farther!

p. 87 (my italics)

The 'gorge', evidently, is an image of the vagina, of the strait gate
through which those who wish truly for freedom must pass. Jane is
aware that freedom means suffering, and confinement means calm;

freedom means risking loss of caste and respectability, even of sinking—for her generation, the horror of horrors—into the squalid depths of the 'fallen woman'. She admits that she 'was not heroic enough to purchase liberty at the price of caste' (p.27); but she is also woman enough to be conscious of her need of a man, a 'master'. Her strong erotic consciousness is shown in the imagery of the water-colours she paints and describes to her reader; no wonder that she can say 'to paint them was to enjoy one of the keenest pleasures I have ever known' (p. 127). Her veins tingle when Mr Rochester comes home, too; when the place leaps into life on acquiring a 'master', when fires glow in the grates and life takes on a more urgent pace. For Jane likes men, particularly square-built, dark, stern, beetle-browed men like the Byronic Mr Rochester. For 'what man' (perceptively asked Lewes) 'could *so* have drawn Rochester?' As Kate Millett writes in *Sexual Politics*, 'Brontë is perhaps the first woman who ever admitted in print that women find men beautiful'. Charlotte Brontë is indeed an essential point of reference in the debate about women's liberation. Jane helps Rochester to control his horse when he slips on the ice in the lane; she helps him too when, a felled giant, he marries her after the house fire which breaks his body and nearly his spirit; and she watches lovingly as he recognizes in the son she has just borne him the colour of his own maimed eyes.

What a tonic for male vanity the conclusion of this book is! We may not be handsome, we may be brusque and rather graceless, but what devotion we can inspire! Lowood was a prison to Jane, scarcely less absolutely so, than the house of her cruel foster-mother in which she grew up; Thornfield was a prison at first, as we have seen, but Ferndean (her home after she has married the man who is her master in more senses than one) is a delight, a place of perpetual honeymoon. 'No woman was ever nearer to her mate than I am', Jane writes at the end, 'ever more absolutely bone of his bone and flesh of his flesh' (pp. 445-6). She has found her true freedom, she says, in her husband's companionship: 'to be together is for us to be . . . as free as in solitude . . .' Love has made her a slave—a willing slave—to an invalid, and she rejoices in her chains. And it is quite evident why. Rochester's infirmities, though severe, do not affect him sexually, and Jane's love for him—as she made clear when describing her agony of moral conflict when he asked her to live with him as his mistress once the fact of his previous marriage had come to light—her love for him is as much erotic as spiritual. Her inability to marry St. John Rivers, the aspirant missionary, is due in large part to the fact that she cannot feel any desire for him, nor he for her, and she realizes that if she lived with him as his wife 'the imprisoned flame' of her ill-directed sexuality would consume her, 'vital after vital' (p. 403).

This is the crux—*the imprisoned flame*. The 'flame' is passion-for-life, usually expressed in the form of an erotic urge to be mastered, dominated, possessed, fertilized; and the 'imprisoned' arises when the 'flame' is thwarted or denied. Such a woman habitually sees herself as a flame yearning to burn freely; but the freedom does not imply licence or promiscuity, or the right to lead the dance, but on the contrary submission to an admired man, a father-figure, someone who is loved in constancy and trusted in fidelity. 'I didn't want to marry and then to have affairs like Louise, my sister', says Margaret Drabble's heroine; 'I wanted to be a one-man girl, and faithful' *(A Summer Bird-Cage,* Penguin ed., p. 188). The more uninhibited liberationists may sneer at this, but opinion surveys show that the majority of women feel the same: they accept the paradox that they long for freedom only to serve the more faithfully a man of their choice. They desire fulfilment, but fulfilment ultimately implies sexual and biological fulfilment, that is, mating and babies: and these bring their own servitude, usually accepted cheerfully enough. Perhaps this is what Jane Eyre is dimly yearning for when, at Lowood School, she cries out into the evening air, 'grant me at least a new servitude!' (p. 87).

In other words, such women want freedom and dignity, but they do not usually envisage these values independently of marriage and child-rearing, which temper them and act as inevitable constraints. Margaret Drabble's heroine knows in her bones that she will marry Francis (the boy she had fallen in love with during her last year at Oxford) once he gets back from his postgraduate year at Harvard. That is why she is making no serious attempt to start a career, despite her First in finals. Her simile for describing her feelings about Francis is significant: 'I felt as though he carried me around in his pocket' (p. 73), and she writes this unresentfully, even joyfully. She accepts her condition as being that of a woman 'inseparably in love', and so does Jane Eyre, who confides proudly, as every reader of fiction knows, in one of the simplest and most dignified sentences in women's literature: 'Reader, I married him'. She has accepted the 'new servitude' she longed for, but she does so, the reader notes, on her own terms: not as Rochester's mistress, but as his wife, and not as a penniless governess, but as an independent woman of means. 'In Jane Eyre', Geoffrey

Wagner has written, 'Charlotte depicted the complete equal. For when the wife is such with her husband as Jane was at the end with Rochester, she forms part of a mutual imagination, and can create herself as submissive if she so desires and requires'.

Another woman who is sympathetically shown coming to terms with her condition is the subject of an impressive Indian novel. Kamala Markandaya's *Two Virgins* (1973) is one of those unpretentious books which require a little time to make their impact: their unique perfume, as it were, is of the slow-release variety. *Two Virgins* is deceptively simple, but its author is an experienced South Indian writer, now living in London, and there is nothing parochial or naïve about the book. It opens on a rather low key, and gradually rises to a climax; the only exciting action is reserved for the last fifty pages. But the slow climb of the dramatic interest is skilfully managed, and the beginning linked to the end with a deftness that can only have come with long study.

'Chingleput ran the only sweetshop in the village' is the sentence with which Miss Markandaya starts her narrative. It is only on the third page that one of the two virgins of the title, Saroja, is introduced in her capacity as one of Chingleput's customers; but on the second page we read this: 'the sugar he drew up on the ends of his tin prongs came up as fine, people said, as maiden's hair'. The subtle patterning of the novel's imagery is discreetly launched in this unobtrusive sentence. Saroja, ferocious but uneasy virgin to the last, sees her maidenhood gently if unsuccessfully tried by Chingleput (who is otherwise a minor character in the story) on the very last page.

The other virgin of the title is Saroja's elder and more beautiful sister Lalitha, but *she* does not remain a virgin for long. She runs away to the big city with a film director, returns pregnant, and is carried back there by her indignant parents who insist that the seducer extricate her from the trouble he has got her into. Saroja, who is dragged everywhere by the family in case she succumbs to the same temptation, is far more upset by the abortion than Lalitha, who on the whole is pleased to be rid of a nuisance. But even the distress Saroja feels is not one permanently to affect her. After Chingleput 'nuzzles her body' with his 'hard organ' she draws away from him. She was not frightened, we are told, 'she knew too much, she had gone through too much to be afraid of anything'. As she rides away, girlishly, on her 'bike', she feels the tears 'cascading down her face', but she does not know for whom they are falling: 'for her, or Chingleput, or for what was ended'. And 'after a while she didn't try. She thought instead of when she was older, felt the wind on her face and the tears drying as she skimmed down the path that led past the fields to the house'.

Lalitha meanwhile has disappeared, has blended in with the wicked city she cannot part from and, in terms at least of the morality according to which she was raised, is a lost creature. Perhaps she will make good, as a film-star or a model; perhaps she will drift into prostitution, though the author implies that she is too canny for that. But Saroja has learned from her sister's experiences, and she, we feel, will turn out all right. When she is ready she will give herself up to the sexual whirlwind which has swept her sister away and has already brushed Saroja herself with its hot breath; but she will master its force, and grow into a mature woman who knows and who controls.

This penetrating study of the awakening of sexuality in a young girl (who, like Ernestina in *The French Lieutenant's Woman*, had 'seen animals couple, and the violence haunted her mind') is also a sensitive account of the impact on a rural community of city mores. Mr Gupta, the 'Western punk' who 'dishonours' Lalitha, drives around in a big car in a village more attuned to the bicycle or the bullock-cart as a mode of transportation. The girls' father, who lives upon the legend of his activities as a terrorist in the independence struggle against Britain, is intimidated and overawed by the city and by Mr Gupta's imposing domestic establishment. All the tensions Satyajit Ray explores in his more recent films, such as *Company Limited*, are discreetly in evidence in this book. How can India develop her economy and raise the standard of living of her people without compromising the standards which give her traditional way of life its honour and dignity? Saroja would seem to point the way. It is possible, Miss Markandaya suggests, to be a woman, to be Indian, to fulfill oneself sexually and personally, without sacrificing all that is good and decent in one's upbringing. It is true we leave Saroja on the threshold of this adventure; but a more positive assertion would have been out of place in a novel of understatement and muted rhetoric such as this.

Writing of this quality serves to point up the vapid falseness of what is thought of by some people as women's fiction *par excellence:* the whole sub-genre of 'romantic' stories, such as those produced by Barbara Cartland, Georgette Heyer, Violet Winspear and other so-called 'lady novelists'. One novel which, while ostensibly subscribing to their values, in fact corrodes them effectively and with great subtlety from within, is that classic of female erotica, *Story of O* (1954). Pauline

Réage is the official name of the author, but it is still a mystery who lies concealed behind the pseudonym. Some think it is Jean Paulhan, who signs the preface; Georges Bataille was in the habit of writing prefaces, signed by his public name, to the erotic novels he published under a pseudonym, but Bataille's was a male pseudonym. If Paulhan or any other man, or group of men, wrote *Histoire d'O*, they carried out a brilliant piece of pastiche which is so like the real thing as not to invalidate the argument I wish to base upon the book. But my feeling, after several readings of the novel, is that it is the authentic work, never to be repeated, of a non-literary woman. The style, though intensely poetic in some parts, is in others clumsy and untutored, and the plot perfunctory; Paulhan would hardly have written like that, even in pursuance of a literary hoax. Then there are the long passages about make-up, clothes and flowers, about women's sexual feelings towards their own bodies, or towards other women in all-female society (a 'gynécée'), which I do not believe a man could have 'planted' convincingly. And above all, the book is so deadly serious—though not at all solemn—I do not think a male joker could have kept a straight face. I prefer to accept as authentic the blurb's quotation from a statement (entitled *Une Fille amoureuse*) attributed to the author herself: 'Who am I, asks Pauline Réage, if not the silent, secret and nocturnal half of someone who has never betrayed herself publicly by any act, gesture or even word, but who communicates via the hidden paths of the imagination with dreams as old as the world itself? Whence did I receive these dreams, in which the purest and most violent love continually permitted, or rather demanded, the most horrifying abandonment, and in which childish visions of chains and whips added to my constraint its own symbols? I cannot tell.' We are all prisoners, she goes on to say, in so far as we all contain within ourselves someone whom we enslave; so that the wild dreams which went to make up her novel were, she found, therapeutic, as long as they told of 'girls in love, prostituted through love, and triumphant in their chains.'

Certainly her heroine, O, cheerfully accepts flagellation and prostitution at the hands of friends and acquaintances merely because her lover René desires it. When he wishes her to become the property of an older English relative of his, Sir Stephen, the very archetype of the strong, silent Curt Jürgens-style hero, she willingly agrees. It is clear that René, though not a homosexual, has a kind of amorous attachment to Sir Stephen which O is happy to assist; if René can please Sir Stephen by giving him O, and if O can please René by submitting to Sir Stephen, then she is happy to do so—and this, even though Sir Stephen treats her with a mixture of old-world courtesy and gutter vulgarity, of gently homage and sadistic brutality. Before he thrashes her within an inch of her life, for instance, he is wont to bow over her hand and kiss it, or to stand back to allow her to pass through doors before him. The predictable happens: René falls in love with a trivial tart, a model called Jacqueline, whom O on their orders lures into their circle, and loses interest in O herself. Such a development a short while before would have broken O's heart, but by now she loves Sir Stephen (who is deeply in love with her too) with an infinitely greater love than she had felt for René, strong as that had seemed at the time. 'There was no pleasure', Miss Réage writes, 'no joy, no imagination to approach the happiness she experienced at the liberty with which Sir Stephen treated her, at the thought that he knew he had to take no care whatever what he did to her, that there was no limit to the ways in which he could take his pleasure upon her body' (Pauvert ed., p. 238). Although she enjoys caressing other women, she cannot conceive of enjoying being made love to by a woman (there is an element of narcissism here of course: she likes to see her own ecstasy mirrored in that which she provokes in other girls); she experiences the highest pitch of sexual bliss only when she is painfully assaulted by the man she loves, or by those he gives her to. She receives her lover 'like a god', and it is in his chains, branded (literally) with his mark, that she feels free. Prostitution dignifies her, captivity fills her with delight, flogging—although a torment while it is being inflicted—she looks back upon with pride.

Naturally, *Story of O* is not a realistic novel—although it has realistic elements, some of them sharp, such as the delightfully catty portrait of Jacqueline—it is an erotic fantasy, even an adult fairy tale, with its 'once upon a time' opening, and not, of course, pornography in the derogatory sense of the term. The language is always decent, even to the point of obscurity in its reluctance to call spades spades, and unlike hard-core pornography is by no means monotonous and repetitive. The story has a genuine development—O's increasing submission to, and love for, Sir Stephen, which reaches its climax when she accepts being paraded at a fashionable dance dressed only in the mask of an owl, branded on the buttocks and chained by the vulva. (The present ending is, of course, the only one possible. A later sequel, 'Return to Roissy', represents, according to Miss Réage herself, the deliberate 'degradation' of *Story of O*, and so 'can never be incorporated'. This additional chapter is more realistic, thus more pornographic, less erotic and less suggestive. O becomes a common prostitute employed in a country-club type of exclusive brothel. Sir Stephen disappears from her life, after embroiling her with a Belgian who is murdered in circumstances which get O involved briefly with the police.)

Nevertheless, some readers may well be shocked, even today, to read the story of a girl who enjoys humiliation and rape, but Pauline Réage does not ask them to take it literally. O does not really walk the streets of Paris, demurely dressed but free of underwear, eternally available to those who can read the sign constituted by the iron ring on her wedding finger; no Paris fashion studio is run by an attractive and efficient woman like O who, under her correct skirt and blouse, bears the sores of recent vicious whippings; no police mortuary is likely to receive a female cadaver flogged into lifelessness and mysteriously branded S.H. on the behind, and betraying signs of recent sodomy and rape. No, *Story of O* is a fantasy; it is a myth, and a stirring and powerful one, of the eternally available, eternally compliant Eve. O in other words is the stuff of our dreams: for men, the dream that they have a woman in their power on whom they can freely inflict their lusts, of whatever kind (short of coprophagia and one or two other perversions about which Miss Réage is understandably not enthusiastic); for women, the fantasy that they are possessed by a daemon lover who shows no mercy and renders them delirious with pleasure and pain. To those who would sneeringly or angrily dismiss such a book there can only be one answer: tremble, ye righteous, for these are your night-thoughts.

For, different as it may at first appear, this book resembles *Jane Eyre* in more ways than one. Both are about female passion, about the way a normally constituted and healthy woman 'melts' in the arms of a strong man; although she would undoubtedly be shocked by a horse-whipping, Jane is clearly not averse to a little rough treatment. Sisters under the skin, both heroines fall deeply and hopelessly in love with men who, though old enough to be their fathers, are still possessed of evident virility. And both heroines find that servitude—in Jane's case to a forceful invalid, in O's to an imperious aristocrat—represents for them the truest and most genuine freedom. And, last but not least, both novels are erotic fantasies written largely for women to read, and dream by.

The same imagery of cage and prison which runs through *Jane Eyre*, through *Histoire d'O* and through *A Summer Bird-Cage*—of cages gladly inhabited, once the owner of the cage is felt to be acceptable—runs also through Sylvia Plath's poignant novel, *The Bell Jar*. As Esther's nervous breakdown develops, she feels more and more that she is enclosed within a cage or a glass jar. The claustrophobia of the suburb in which she spends the summer of her breakdown is palpable, and the monotony of sterile day following sterile day is powerfully rendered. Like Margaret Drabble's heroine, she feels her 'social loneliness', due to the 'dislocation that', according to Miss Drabble's Sarah, 'girls of my age and lack of commitments feel' (p. 96). This is the dilemma of the intelligent woman. Neither Sarah nor Esther can subsist on a facile happiness such as their sisters or friends seem content with. Sarah sees herself as 'crouching inside the walls of [her] consciousness' (p.80); for Esther it is 'sitting under the glass bell jar, stewing in my own sour air' (Faber ed., p. 196). The solution for Sarah, after a false trail or two, is to determine to marry her Oxford sweetheart: for Esther, to lose her virginity by the good offices of a maths professor. This heralds her recovery, and her freedom. She first casts off all her old associations, her mother whom she detests, her friends, the maths professor whom she amusingly forces to foot the bill for the emergency medical attention made necessary by the hemorrhage which follows her deflowering; and then, she says, 'I was perfectly free', and safely out of the bell jar. The freedom is rather like that of Stephen Dedalus when he calls to his defence the only arms he allows himself: 'silence, exile and cunning.' It is freedom to seek the *grand large*, where perhaps Esther will marry. She certainly thinks about marriage: 'of course I didn't know who would marry me now that I'd been where I had been', she says (p. 254), referring to the mental hospital; but she is clearly not too worried that someone, somewhere will find her attractive enough notwithstanding.

In spite of the fact that Esther 'hated the idea of serving men in any way' (p. 79), and that Miss Plath's novel is one in which men do not cut a very impressive figure, this heroine, as much as the others, is held within her condition. She feels her virginity is a millstone round her neck: 'it had been of such enormous importance to me for so long that my habit was to defend it at all costs', she says: 'I had been defending it for five years and I was sick of it' (pp. 240-1). Once she is rid of it she can 'smile into the dark' because she feels 'part of a great tradition' (p. 242). The female condition, in other words, is one which it is ultimately an act of freedom to assume voluntarily rather than fight against. This the wisest of the women's liberationists freely accept. 'It is necessary', writes Simone ae Beauvoir in *The Second Sex*, 'that by and through their natural differentiation men and women unequivocally affirm their brotherhood'. A woman's existential choice, in other words, is to accept her nature with pride and dignity, escaping out of the cage of her conditioned fears into a world where she will seek not to oust and destroy men, but to live with them in partnership and brotherhood.

For to apply the colonial or class struggle analogy to the campaign for women's rights is a mistake. A colonial people can live without their foreign masters; that is why they can expel them, ultimately, with impunity. The proletariat cannot manage so easily without the entrepreneurial and intellectual skills of the bourgeoisie, which is perhaps why there has never been a truly proletarian revolution which has survived more than a few days. But it is said that women cannot normally live without men for more than a few months, nor men without women for more than a few weeks. Our sexual makeup forces us willy-nilly into alliance. Too often in the past that alliance has been based on subjugation and domination, which is mythified in the *Histoire d'O* situation. But it need not always be like that. Jane Eyre, in the end, knew a happy partnership, and Margaret Drabble's Sarah looks forward to one with Francis when he returns; she will be a don's wife, but not his inferior, partly because Francis would not wish that, but mainly because, thanks largely to the efforts of women's liberationists in the past, Sarah has gone to university on equal terms with men and gained first-class honours in the same examinations which they take. Sylvia Plath's Esther will not always know the solitude and isolation of the bell jar. And even O, in the midst of her humiliation, was never an inferior: she was free to go at any time, free to cut off her chains, free to fly out of the cage whose bars only existed in her imagination and that of her lovers. She was held captive because her slavery was willed, self-assumed. Of course this is no formula for everyday living; *Histoire d'O* is erotic fantasy, as I have stressed, and Miss Réage would no doubt be the last person to wish to live as O does. But that is the attraction of literature: it doesn't have to be true. We can use it, as Miss Réage does, to indulge fantasies we would not seriously wish to see fulfilled. As dreams, they do her—and her readers—good. We emerge from the bizarre goings-on at the Chateau de Roissy into the calm light of day, into a world in which girls, fortunately, are not branded and tortured, in which they can express their love for men in less extreme ways. But it is good to have such an exemplary love-story, even if we must take it all with a pinch of salt. I myself do not think it is a question, as Kate Millett would argue, that 'this intensity of humiliation constitutes identity for those who despise themselves' (p. 18). It is, rather, a form of extreme poetry of love, of adoration, of peace; it is, at the same time, an affirmation of dignity, of the unconquered, inviolate self which continues untrammelled and unscathed:

> She was nothing more than watching wakefulness and night... In a week she learned fear, but also certainty; anguish, but also happiness. René threw himself on her like a buccaneer on his prisoner, and she became a prisoner with joy... Every night spent with René was for her a night for ever... What repose, what delight was to be found in the iron ring which pierces the flesh and weighs it down for all time, the brand which can never be erased, the hand of a master which reclines you upon a bed of rock, the master's adoration which can seize without pity that which it loves to enjoy...
>
> pp. 73, 129, 133, 233

At this point (blasphemously perhaps) one is tempted to murmur, after Dante, that this adoration truly is *l'amor che move il sole e l'altre stelle*, the love that moves the sun and the other stars.

CHAPTER SEVEN

Images and Promises in the Western Sky

Images and Promises
in the Western Sky

*America is a land of wonders, in which everything
is in constant motion and every change seems an
improvement*

ALEXIS DE TOQUEVILLE

1

This chapter deals with one aspect of a much larger topic—the quest
for a mythical promised land. In Chapter 2 we looked at one novel, *Le
Grand Meaulnes* by Alain-Fournier, which is concerned with the
search for an imaginary lost domain within a familiar country. My
subject here is a real place: the continent which Henry James, a great
transatlantic voyager, called 'this well-wooded corner of the Western
world, where the sunsets [are] so beautiful and one's ambitions [are] so
pure', and whose visitors, like Felix in *The Europeans,* can declare it 'a
paradise', entirely free of the 'misery' left behind 'over there—beyond
the sea'. I am referring, of course, to the United States of America,
source and haven of that splendid myth of hope and possibility, the
American Dream. James's *The Europeans* is a novel largely about the
promises America holds out for the European mind, though explored of
course with irony; besides, James only deals with 'aristocratic'
Americans and well-born Europeans, not with the recently-arrived
citizen or immigrant riff-raff. Although his is a rather partial
view—dealing (unlike Kafka's and Céline's, which we shall come to in
a moment) with a civilized if provincial world—James is still writing
about a mythical land, much as later novelists do; it is interesting to·
compare Eugenia's largely empty-handed return home with the
richer, if intangible, exports of Evelyn Waugh's later hero. What
Henry James shows, unlike the others, is European 'sophistication'
corrupting American 'simplicity', or at the least in danger of doing so;
though his attitude to America became, not unnaturally, a good deal

149

less Edenic after a visit, following an absence of twenty years, in 1904–1905, which he recorded in his book of 1907, *The American Scene*. With even later works by other writers, the boot is very much on the other foot; but any discussion of this topic must start with early James, who was not boasting when he said that it is 'impossible to an outsider to say whether I am at a given moment an American writing about England or an Englishman writing about America'. (In this chapter I shall be concerned chiefly with Englishmen and other Europeans writing about America, but with an occasional sideglance where relevant at one or two Americans writing about their own country and particularly about the myth it projects.)

Henry James's comparative view of Europe and America is reflected and endorsed in a recent study in literary nostalgia and anachronism, John Fowles's *The French Lieutenant's Woman*. Fowles's narrator, like James's, shows his Victorian hero noticing during a visit to the United States a 'certain lack of the finer shades of irony', but feeling himself compensated by his discovery of a 'frankness, a directness of approach, a charming curiosity that accompanied the open hostility: a naïvety, perhaps, yet with a face that seemed delightfully fresh-complexioned after the farded culture of Europe'. In common with other visitors he finds American women 'more freely spoken than their European contemporaries', but like them, too, he finds 'their forwardness very attractive'. Fowles intervenes to explain that his hero's feelings were perhaps not very different from those an Englishman might experience in the United States at the present time: he would find, Fowles tells us, 'so much that repelled, so much that was good; so much chicanery, so much honesty; so much brutality and violence, so much concern and striving for a better society' (Panther ed., pp. 371-2). In this passage Fowles offers not only a Jamesian view of the contrast between old-world tired sophistication and new-world spontaneous freshness, but also a twentieth-century angle on the contradictions and hopes enshrined in the American dream. These are the twin themes which I shall be exploring further in the course of this chapter.

Both continents have of course traditionally used each other to define to themselves their own specific identity, and Henry James is an important figure in this development; but it is not the American image of Europe which concerns me here, but rather the old world's mythic involvement with that land of boundless potential into which it ejected millions of its undesirables, those it would not tolerate and those it could not feed; the very people, of course, who then proceeded to assist in the construction of the American achievement, to write home about it, and to encourage countless more to abandon the attempt to carve a hope for themselves at home, and to face instead the risks and opportunities of the new-found land where men could say with the simplicity of truth—as they do in *The Europeans*—'we are all princes here'. Before going on, it would be as well to attempt a definition of the phenomenon which has become known as 'the American Dream'.

Lionel Trilling is quite correct when he states that his 'is the only nation that prides itself upon a dream and gives its name to one, "the American Dream" '. The application of the term 'dream' to the American experiment seems first to have been made by Henry Adams in 1884. Later, James Truslow Adams wished to call his best-known work, *The Epic of America*, by the even more heroic title of *The American Dream*, but his publisher rejected the suggestion on the grounds that book buyers would 'never pay $3 for a "dream" '. Later on, evidently, the publishers of Edward Albee's play *The American Dream* and Norman Mailer's novel *An American Dream* did not share such misgivings. Lionel Trilling might have added that the United States has been uniquely successful in persuading other nations to share in its 'dream', to believe in it to such an extent that even the most illiterate peasant in the most remote village of the Old World was eventually infected by its potent magic. For the American dream, according to David Potter, was a dream of 'absolute equality and of universal opportunity', and an 'ideal of freedom', a hope held out simultaneously to the oppressed, the persecuted, the starving and the deprived; to those who lacked any or all of Roosevelt's famous 'four freedoms'—freedom of speech and of religion, freedom from want and from fear. The Statue of Liberty, let us not forget, faces eastwards: towards Europe. The intellectual harried for his politics, the Jew hounded for his race, the dissenter persecuted for his religion all jostled on Ellis Island with the unemployed labourer and the dispossessed peasant awaiting admittance to the country which promised to leave them in peace to think and say what they liked, or to feed, clothe and house them to previously unimagined standards of comfort, provided they were prepared to accept whatever job they could find and work hard at it. It may have been a country which provided no 'free lunch', but it was a place where those who once wore rags could dress 'like a doctor or a merchant in the old country', and those who had been lucky back home if they could fill their bellies with lentils or potatoes were now able to afford steak for breakfast. These points were made by Alistair Cooke in his successful television series on America—since an equally successful book, of especial interest since Cooke is himself a former immigrant from Britain and broadcasts home regularly on American affairs. But the American dream, like all ideals, bumped up of course against some glaring contradictions, not least among them the fact that there is inherent within it a conflict between the Adamic or backward-looking tendency, and the Utopian or forward-looking impulse. It may be this basic dichotomy which accounts for inconsistencies at the practical level, starting with the notorious fact that Jefferson, who drafted the document which magnificently asserts the inalienable right of man to liberty, was himself in 1776 an owner of slaves; it did of course disturb Americans themselves that the 'land of the free' imposed servitude within its own borders, to the extent of becoming one of the main causes of the Civil War. Such contradictions have continued right up to the present day, when the Red Indian and the Black are bringing several unwelcome birds home to roost, when abundance appears to mean in practice that the individual is induced by massive advertising not to get what he wants, but to like what he gets, and when saturation bombing has been the expression of an altruistic wish to make other nations share in the American Dream. Such contrasts are not of course the monopoly of the United States, but as Alistair Cooke points out, 'in America they always seem more depressing and dramatic, because America didn't inherit a nation: it invented one and boasted that it would be better than everything that had gone before'.

Nevertheless the dream was no illusion, and the vast majority who braved the miseries of the immigrant ships and the petty harassments of immigration officials were successful in making it to the better life they longed for (if not exactly to the Eden which Columbus sets out to discover in Michel de Ghelderode's sardonic play of 1927, *Christopher Columbus*). It is, after all, a plain and simple fact that Jews escaping pogroms or Irishmen fleeing the potato famine not only saved their skins, but joined in the building of a nation which has been able to guarantee its inhabitants the highest standard of living in the world. What other lottery has granted such dividends to those prepared to stake their all upon it? Violence, with other unpleasant features, may constitute ingredients of the American apple-pie, but the pie still tastes good. The darker side of the American experience—as projected by Dreiser in *An American Tragedy* or in Norman Mailer's nightmarish vision of the myth called *An American Dream*—is of course a serious drawback, the dream turned sour. But as David Madden has said, 'it is often those who want to believe in the Dream, but most intensely see the impossibility of making it come true, who wish to see the Dream immolated in Nightmare'. Edward Albee has similarly aimed his play *The American Dream* at what he calls the 'fiction that everything in this slipping land of ours is peachy-keen.' Books—both from within and from without America—with titles like 'The Air-Conditioned Nightmare' and 'The Jungle of Cities', are highly expressive in this connection. The famous Norwegian writer Knut Hamsun published his rather jaundiced views about the United States in a book called *The Cultural Life of Modern America*, and before him, of course, Charles Dickens's *American Notes* had expressed similar reservations about the country. Not all writers have seen it that way, not even all American writers: *The Great Gatsby* ends with this splendid celebration of the American Dream, held up in healthy contrast to the bored and unhappy life of the jazz age depicted in the novel which this passage concludes:

> And as the moon rose higher the inessential houses began to melt away until gradually I became aware of the old island here that flowered once for Dutch sailors' eyes—a fresh, green breast of the new world. Its vanished trees, the trees that had made way for Gatsby's house, had once pandered in whispers to the last and greatest of all human dreams; for a transitory enchanted moment man must have held his breath in the presence of this continent, compelled into an aesthetic contemplation he neither understood nor desired, face to face for the last time in history with something commensurate to his capacity for wonder.

It is this 'capacity for wonder' which even today permits the American tourist authority, without too glaring an incongruity, to place double-page colour advertisements in widely-circulating periodicals in Great Britain such as *Radio Times*, proclaiming 'the Great American Adventure' and calling upon the British to 'come see the wonders of the West—only in America'. Those brave words, 'only in America', still resound across the Atlantic a century after the great migrations of the persecuted and forsaken millions who have helped to make the United States the most powerful country in the world, a land where 'prophecy and nostalgia meet'.

II

And this at a time when the frontier, which Dixon Ryan Fox shrewdly labelled 'the edge of the unused', was perforce ceasing to be 'the great image of the American sense of possibility' as projected by Fenimore Cooper and Mark Twain, and first documented by the historian Frederick Jackson Turner, who believed that America was 'another name for opportunity'. While it existed, the frontier symbolized the seemingly infinite potential of the United States. First, in Vermont, the English created a little England; later, in Wisconsin, the Germans made a little Germany; but they also established a new land, and a new hope. As Robert B. Heilman has noted, 'dreams about America are an import from Europe'. Refugees and immigrants wrote novels—such as Ole Rölvaag's *Giants in the Earth*, and Abraham Cahan's *The Rise of David Levinsky*—which chronicled, usually without irony, the epic of the opening up of America by her newest citizens; *Giants in the Earth* is about the bleak and hostile spirit of the Dakota prairie mastered by a heroic Norwegian pioneer who dies in a snowstorm, 'his eyes set toward the west', and *The Rise of David Levinsky* tells how a poor Jewish boy from Russia lifts himself from the lowest depths of poverty (he arrived in America, he tells us, with four cents in his pocket) to a position in the cloak and suit trade which earned him a fortune of two million dollars, though this money, he informs us sadly, was not able to purchase for him the happiness in marriage he craved most of all. These books (and many others, such as Johan Bojer's *The Emigrants* on which Jan Troell's film of the same title was based) have been followed in more recent times by such works as *America America* by the film-maker Elia Kazan, which celebrates the 'golden shore' of the immigrant's promised land and shows how for the novel's Greek hero, 'America represented a sanctuary to which no Overlord would set the torch'; this 'exigency of choice', the novel demonstrates, has been a primary motive behind many waves of European emigration to the United States. Even more recently, *Double or Nothing* by Raymond Federman tells graphically how the belly of the woman whom the hero makes love to soon after his arrival in the United States, appears to him like 'the belly of America' herself.

Works by native born Americans like Carson McCullers and Irwin Shaw also project the immigrant's viewpoint. In 'The Aliens', a short story by Carson McCullers, a refugee Jew is travelling southwards on a Greyhound bus to Lafayetteville where he intends to establish a home and bring over his family; 'behind him', the narrator suggests, 'was an abyss of anxious wandering, suspense, of terror and of hope'. More coarsely, Irwin Shaw's novel *Rich Man, Poor Man*, announced by the publishers as being 'about the American dream', speaks of 'the top', where one's arrival 'is greeted with hosannahs and Cadillacs by earlier arrivals'. For McCullers, the American dream is about freedom from fear, whereas for Shaw it has much more to do with success of the most basely material kind. Though crudely projected in *Rich Man, Poor Man*, the idea is not in itself disreputable. John F. Kennedy was not too proud to remark, during a sentimental journey to Ireland in 1963, that had his great-grandfather not emigrated (carrying with him 'a strong religious faith and a strong desire for liberty'), the future President of the United States 'would be working at the Albatross Company across the road'. This constituted, if ever anything did, a double win on the lottery I referred to earlier.

Someone who did not hit either jackpot was the Swedish-American labour leader Joe Hill, executed in the promised land in 1915, and since lovingly brought to life again by Bo Widerberg in the movie of the same title. This film is of course influenced to a large extent by the current fashion in anti-Americanism which flourishes in Americanized Sweden, but other artists have not disdained to hoist the United States with their own petard. In *After Many a Summer*, Aldous Huxley amuses himself poking rather heartless fun through his spokesman-hero at the contradictions between the American ideal of democracy and the reality of big business dictator-bosses, who build air-conditioned all-electric Gothic castles, while *Grapes of Wrath*-style transients from the Kansas dustbowl slave for a bare living in the Californian orange-groves which stretch below. The novel tells the story of an American plutocrat who refuses to grow old and commissions grotesque experiments to find the elixir which will prevent him from aging. Huxley stresses the tragic aspect of the American dream, the death that is an inescapable threat to its illusions of permanent happiness. A decade later Evelyn Waugh explored the same topic in his 'Anglo-American tragedy', *The Loved One*, a book of flippant and even facile satire directed at a horror-California, combining all the enormities which offended Waugh's fastidious tastes, principally American girls, each packaged like the 'standard product' and fulfilling 'prescribed rites' when preparing for a date, such as 'dabbing herself under the arms with a preparation designed to seal the sweat glands'.

The superior sneer is never far behind writing of this sort; one wonders sometimes whether it is not provoked by British envy of an ex-colony which has made it to leadership of the free world. Henry James's story 'An International Episode' (1878) is a bitingly cool critique of such British snobbery, of an arrogant conviction of superiority over a 'colonial' people with allegedly no 'leisured class'; a patronizing attitude so deep-rooted in the insular consciousness that not even a lord's passion for an American girl will shake it.

But the British novels of the inter-war generation of writers—so witty, so urbane, so clever, but so restricted in ambition, so parochial in tone, so frivolous in essence in spite of (or perhaps because of) their would-be seriousness of social commentary—such novels are not characteristic of the best and most valid British reaction to the American Dream, as I hope to show. And before all this, Anthony Trollope, Charles Dickens, Matthew Arnold and D.H. Lawrence, though by no means uncritical, had had the magnanimity to recognise the positive achievements of American civilization; that the poor 'are not abject in their poverty' (Trollope), that the nation had phoenix-like the 'power of springing from the ashes of its faults and its vices' (Dickens), that the women possess 'the charm of a natural manner' (Arnold), and that the servile habits of obedience never, in the land of the free, outlast the first generation (Lawrence).

III

The 'native' immigrant novel, which showed how, as Turner put it, 'in the crucible of the frontier the immigrants were Americanized and liberated', was copied and even pastiched in Europe by Franz Kafka, who never crossed the Atlantic, and by Louis-Ferdinand Céline, who did. 'The crossing of the seas', Theodore C. Blegen has written, 'and the way west are essential chapters in the international story of the emigrant', a story Kafka took a great interest in and accumulated documentation about. When he began his own version, now known under the title *America*, he was careful to follow the traditional plot. The novel begins with Karl's arrival in New York harbour after being 'packed off to America by his parents because a servant girl had seduced him and got herself with child by him', and proceeds, in the manner both of the picaresque and the Bildungsroman, to take the young hero across country until he winds up in 'The Nature Theatre of Oklahoma', at which point the manuscript abruptly ends. But not before the hero, with the theatre, has begun to move overland and realize 'how huge America is', and how like a rebirth it is for a European to land there. For a story based entirely on second-hand knowledge, *America* is remarkably precise and lucid about the strengths and weaknesses of the American experiment; the girls are beautiful and show ease of manner, developments are rapid and money is quickly made, and an ambitious man has every opportunity to succeed on his own: these in Kafka's eyes are some of the good features of American civilization. Less good are the poverty and overcrowding on the lower East Side and the general roughness of American manners. But on this guide-book version of the U.S.A. Kafka hangs his own characteristic Piranesi-type vision; the complexity of the organization in the hotel Karl works for is a metaphor for the complexity of modern life, and the ramifications of the Oklahoma Theatre appear to be infinite. So much so that Franz Kuna has been moved to conclude that 'despite its title *America* is a novel about Europe'. Indeed, eventually the shrewd 'realistic' observations—about American technology, about the way an immigrant rapidly starts to feel cut off from the homeland which he knows is changing behind him so that return soon becomes impossible—such naturalistic elements fade into insignificance beside the power of the sharply comic tale which is Kafka's private dream upon the American Dream. It incorporates, for all that, the archetypal westward journey, and manages to recreate at a distance some of the experiences and emotions of the real immigrants: Karl comes in search of the American Dream and is more or less satisfied at the end with the way it has turned out.

Céline's *Journey to the End of the Night* is less of a dream and more of a nightmare. The central section of Bardamu's odyssey is set in the U.S.A., but a U.S.A. flattened and distorted by Céline's pessimism concerning the quality of human life, tersely summed up in his remark, 'the bigger the town and the higher the town, the less they bloody well care'. In Céline's eyes America is like any other place: a desert of loneliness and indifference; and Bardamu's journey is a desperate cosmopolitan search doomed to failure there as much as anywhere else. Almost, but not quite. Bardamu, whose experience at Ford's is like an infernal foreshadowing of Chaplin's *Modern Times*, does carry something away with him from the United States: the memory of the only love of his life, the prostitute Molly, whom he contrasts with Lola, the archetypal American tease who figures in the early part of the book.

To Molly Bardamu attributes such redemption as he is ever likely to
know. His trip to the States, only a stage on his long and dolorous
pilgrimage, is thus after all worthwhile, in spite of the horror of those
cruel cities which, Céline believes, dehumanize and craze all who come
within their orbit.

This reaction to the American Dream, extreme as it is, is typical of
French responses, which differ from most others in their refusal to be
impressed. Jean-Paul Sartre, for instance, notes in his American essays
(collected in *Situations III*) that the U.S.A. is a country of the most
violent contrasts, in which the national myths of happiness, freedom
and equality are continually belied by the reality: 'nowhere else
perhaps', he writes, 'will you find such an enormous gap between men
and myths, between life and the collective representation of life'.
There is more than a trace of superior amusement in Sartre's attitude,
but he does concede the country's openness to both adventure and
reform.

More trivial, if more earnest, is Célia Bertin's tourist version in her
novel *Je t'appellerai Amérique* (Paris, 1972). Her comments on the
contrasts between splendour and ugliness do not rise above the
standards of *Elle* journalism, the language of which she handles with
grisly smoothness; Sartre, though frequently slick and even
superficial, is never obtuse as Bertin is. Nearer to a genuine celebration
of the United States is Michel Butor's *Mobile*, subtitled 'Study
Towards a Representation of the United States': it adopts the well-
tried journey formula, but the quest, as in *Lolita*, is now conducted in
an automobile. More 'grainy' as a French reaction to New York is
Claude Simon's novel *Conducting Bodies* (1971). The abrupt changes
of subject in the narrative (the text in a real sense generates itself,
making the novel its own narrator) give a dazzling sense of the frenzy
and pace of urban life in the U.S.A. In comparison, Butor's work is
more leisured, offering a kaleidoscopic vision embracing America in
space and time, giving a sense of its short and violent history and
immense physical distances. Much more fantastic, much more
concerned to capture the mythical quality of America is Alain Robbe-
Grillet's *Project for a Revolution in New York* (1970), which explores
the legend of American violence by imagining Manhattan in ruins and
in the throes of bloody revolution. The upheaval is at once curiously
real and unreal, since it takes place against the background of a
monotonously regular world of subway, fire-escapes, buildings,
streets, the familiar merging imperceptibly with the

extraordinary—and the marvellous with the terrifying—in a manner vaguely reminiscent of Poe. Less subtle, and thus less effective, is Alan Burns's surrealist-collage treatment of the Kennedy story entitled *Dreamerika!* (1972), which attempts through concrete and visual devices to evoke the tensions in the American Dream, but only succeeds in offering a witty ocular joke. A more successful 'pop' evocation of the American Dream is the Australian journalist Clive James's lyric 'Driving Through Mythical America', which Pete Atkin has set to music. Basically a lament for the student victims of the Kent State killings, this poem weaves allusions to American popular culture and consumer durables into the story of the four who set out 'to speak their minds about the war', until their history, 'which had them covered like a gun', hits them 'like a bolt out of the blue'. Clive James's poem both praises America for her cultural achievements in film and other media, and indicts her for her violence and intolerance.

IV

It will be apparent, I think, that this new country—at once self-assured and lacking in confidence, assertive yet guilt-ridden, vulgar yet beautiful, raising at its gates a Statue of Liberty yet burying in its archives the record of witch-hunts from Salem to McCarthy, a land of immense material prosperity where the poor grow poorer, a nation which projects its values brazenly yet feels anxieties about its image—that this country, huge even in the scale of its contradictions, has inevitably provoked reactions in literature as intense as they are mixed. Correspondingly, and not surprisingly, no other land, not even Atlantis or Cathay, has been so fervently mythified by the peoples of the world.

What is especially interesting and curious in this context is the appearance in the last decade or so of what Malcolm Bradbury has called the Jamesian international novel in reverse, in which the European is cast as the innocent abroad, and the journey he undertakes is not eastward, but westward, usually to the 'end of America', the Pacific coast, the definitive frontier. This trip across the United States occurs in very similar circumstances in Vladimir Nabokov's *Lolita*, Malcolm Bradbury's *Stepping Westward* and Bertin's *Je t'appellerai Amérique*. Similar to *Stepping Westward* in their 'innocent Britisher' motif, but lacking the physical transcontinental journey, are Waugh's *The Loved One*, Thomas Hinde's *High*, William Cooper's *Love on the*

Coast, Kingsley Amis's *One Fat Englishman,* and Wilfrid Sheed's *A Middle Class Education.*

The novels by Waugh, Hinde and the others explore the American Dream from a more or less static view-point. For Waugh, the act of setting the novel in southern California, where the infinitude of America's dream and excess is seen at its quintessence, had obvious satirical advantages. Whispering Glades becomes a figure for the U.S.A.—Arcadian, Edenic in an ironic way, a parody of Christopher Columbus's paradisal garden. There are, in addition, aphoristic comments on American life (such as that the secret of social ease is that no one there expects you to listen to what they are telling you), and these observations occur too in *High,* for instance when Peterson lectures his American girl-friend on the folly of her kind in pursuing blindly the ideal of 'perpetual ecstasy'.

But the interest of novels like *Lolita* and *Stepping Westward* is that, unlike those just mentioned, their comment is a dynamic one. The plot involves not only (as the others do) a sexual adventure, but also a fantastic journey across the breadth of the American continent. Nabokov's middle-aged European intellectual takes up with nymphet Lolita and travels with her great distances over an extended period of time. Bradbury's visiting British writer-in-residence (he is invited to a University which the author satirically names Benedict Arnold after a notorious American who betrayed his country to the British) falls in love with Julie, the student, who represents for him the quintessential America which Walker, 'stepping westward' in Wordsworth's phrase, fails ultimately to accommodate with. Similarly Wilfrid Sheed's young Oxford graduate who goes to America on a grant finds it all too much to cope with and makes a mess of things; his sharp and caustic wit is alien to America, from which he retreats in disgrace: 'he didn't understand them', comments the narrator, 'they didn't understand him, nobody understood anything'.

Likewise Célia Bertin's herione, a French woman professor visiting Boston, falls in love with a young student called Michael and travels with him in a Volkswagen to the Californian beaches, a journey in space and time since their affair begins in the depths of a New England winter and ends in the Mediterranean spring of the West Coast. In the case of the novels by Nabokov, Bradbury and Bertin, the loved one—significantly younger than the lover—represents America; and we recall that the first name of Waugh's American heroine is Aimée, literally 'the loved one'. *Lolita*—a great American novel feeding upon roots deep in the Russian tradition of the comic grotesque—is a multi-layered symbolic tale, one major strand of which is a love-affair with America which fails. Significantly, as Bertin's heroine is surprised into surrender by the young man's bold approach which he learned, she discovers later, from an older woman, so Humbert is seduced by a knowing Lolita, and not the other way round. But America having, in the person of its young people, ravished the staid Europeans eventually abandons them. For Nabokov's hero the only outcome of this rejection is vengeance and death; for Bertin's the resigned and unresentful packing of bags for home. In *Stepping Westward* Walker (who, symbolically and true to his name, cannot drive a car) fails sexually with Julie, and his American idyll (which had also included such episodes as cocking a snook at that New World shibboleth, the loyalty oath) comes to an abrupt end. And in *High* the philosophy of the American girl Jill, and the culture she lives in, is shown to be as 'deceptive as a drug trip', and her own version of the American Dream is sardonically described as being equivalent to 'dying in pure orgasm'. The world Thomas Hinde's hero comes up against is too complex for him and he retreats, as do all the others, in failure. Likewise the English liberalism of Bradbury's Walker tries (but fails) to achieve something without hurting people; in fact, Walker does a lot of damage, and returns to England with his tail between his legs, unlike Waugh's hero who carried back, in the concluding words of *The Loved One*, 'the artist's load, a great, shapeless chunk of experience, bearing it home to his ancient and comfortless shore, to work on it hard and long'.

Indeed, *The Loved One* has been shown to be the last of the 'Chuzzlewit' line of English novels: books in which European experience is brought over the Atlantic to expose American innocence. After Waugh, novelists will present matters the other way about; but in his book Europe, even if it is described as 'dying', is still being seen as a 'civilization with sharper needs'. This explains why Dennis the Englishman can only destroy his loved one, Aimée Thanatogenos—her Greek surname means, of course, 'death-engendering'—since her spirit 'was something apart', however standard her Southern Californian accent, sparse her mind, and deodorized her body. This spirit had to be sought, Waugh tells us, in the 'eagle-haunted passes of Hellas':

An umbilical cord of cafés and fruit shops, of ancestral shady businesses (fencing and pimping) united Aimée, all unconscious, to

the high places of her race. As she grew up the only language she
knew expressed fewer and fewer of her ripening needs.

Penguin ed., p. 105

Gradually, under the influence of Dennis and his anthology of
immortal verses, Aimée's incurable cultural alienation obtrudes itself
upon her consciousness; in the watches of the night 'Attic voices'
prompt her to a higher destiny than that of her immediate and
renegade forbears, the father who frequented the Four Square Gospel
Temple and the mother who drank. The voices Aimée hears speak to
her not of Los Angeles's chapels and speakeasies, but of the Minotaur,
of Agamemnon turning his eyes away from the sacrifice of his daughter
Iphigenia, and of Alcestis and proud Antigone. She injects herself with
poison and literally engenders her own death.

After *The Loved One* the implications of Waugh's vision — which
Malcolm Bradbury has described as 'American innocence turned
bland and mechanical, European experience turned anarchic,
decadent and death-centred' — are worked out in a number of novels
which all have in common what Nabokov would call their 'invention'
of America, and concretize their complex attraction-repulsion
syndrome *vis-à-vis* the American Dream in the symbol of an intense,
passionate, lyrical but doomed sexual encounter. The love affair is a
metaphor — seen at its most elaborate and intricate in *Lolita,* which is
by far the most aesthetically complex of these books — of the agonising
attempt to come to grips with the American Dream itself. Lolita is the
true daughter of the American Dream: the boy and the other girls
concerned are likewise symbols of the United States as a whole, for
they are bright, naïve, fresh, self-confident, beautiful, available; but
sooner or later they disappoint the expectations of lovers originating
from older, more blasé, more experienced and refined cultures. So in
the end like returns to like: Walter to his cosy British wife, Julie to her
American man, and Lolita becomes Mrs Richard F. Schiller. For
Humbert, the *émigré* with the 'horrible careful English', the outcome,
tragically, can only be his own death, for he has failed in his attempt to
reincarnate, in Lolita the American, his first love, his European
Annabel Lee. Humbert, like Nabokov's other character Pnin, has
nowhere to retreat to, nowhere else to go; Pnin's Russian homeland has
been swept away by the whirlwind, and there can be no return. Like
Kafka's hero, Humbert cannot afford to be distracted by idle thoughts
of home; if he cannot come to terms with the American Dream,

symbolized by its females (which Sean O'Faolain once described as being 'as intoxicating a creation as a flight of pink flamingos'), he has no other hope. Humbert is a kind of scapegoat, therefore, whose failure in America is offered to placate the fates and permit his less benighted countrymen to be taken to the bosom of the home of the brave. The heroes of most European novels, on the other hand, can renounce the American Dream and leave God's own country without too much regret, because it is not the basis of their value systems and because they are able to retain what Karl and Humbert must sever, their bloodlink with what D.H. Lawrence would call the 'spirit of their place': Europe's ancient and not really *so* comfortless a shore. For impressed as they undoubtedly are by the American Dream, in their bones they feel just like Henry James's Eugenia who declared on the deck of the ship which was bearing her home: 'Europe seems to me much larger than America'. She was not referring, it hardly needs saying, to their comparative acreages.

CHAPTER EIGHT

Novel and Reader, Fiction and Man

CHAPTER EIGHT

Novel and Reader,
Fiction and Man

*What is a novelist but a general who sends his
troops across fields of paper?*

NORMAN MAILER

I

The reader of fiction may be forgiven if he feels occasionally like
throwing up his hands in despair at the amorphous, even anarchic
quality the form of the novel not infrequently shows. There are
moreover moments, writes Dan Jacobson (himself a novelist), in
which 'habitual readers of novels have experienced spells when they
have found that the conventions of the form suddenly appear paltry,
tiresome, and even disgusting', when they rebel against what he calls
the 'slow and cumbersome machinery' and 'something irredeemably
stubborn and stupid about the form'. 'Who needs these made-up
stories?' the sceptical reader may be driven to ask; 'aren't there enough
real stories in the world without our having to trouble ourselves with
fictions?' We appear, on the one hand, to have a form — that of the
novel — which is mercurial and elusive to a fault, and on the other to be
presented with a series of conventions which if one allows oneself to be
over-exposed to them can become tedious in the extreme. Anyone who
has undertaken a crash course in novel-reading, as have some students
reading for higher degrees in universities, will vouch for the fact that
too concentrated an exposure to fictions can weary the brain. But then
so can too great an indulgence in the so-called 'facts' of television
journalism, radio bulletins and newspapers. It is then that we return to
novels because, to quote Jacobson again, 'they make it a little more
difficult for us to bed ourselves down in an insulating nest of public

preoccupations; in their concern with individual consciousness, in their humiliating circumstantiality, they come too close to home. Paradoxically,' he concludes, 'one can say that they are too "real" ' (*The Listener*, 30 May 1968, p. 693).

How 'real' novels are is, of course, the subject of much debate; what is not in dispute is that the novel is always a narrative, a tale told from a specific point of view. 'Point of view' is a term much used in the theory of fiction; although a large number of points of view have been distinguished by some critics, there are basically only two: first person and third person narration. (Michel Butor's virtuoso use of the formal second person *'vous'* in his novel *Second Thoughts*, 1957, is an idiosyncratic and isolated exception). Narration from the first-person viewpoint has some obvious advantages: it enables the author without artificiality to enter the intimacy of the protagonist's mind and betray its most secret thoughts and feelings. But there are serious drawbacks to this form of narration: if access to the hero is privileged and extensive, by the same token (since we are not able to read the minds of other people), the thoughts and feelings of the other characters must remain a matter of conjecture to hero, author and reader alike. Needless to say some novelists turn this opaqueness to good ironic account (*The Outsider* by Albert Camus relies heavily, as we have seen, on the inscrutability of other people). The third person is, however, the more natural and widespread mode of narration, and most novelists have assumed it grants them licence to virtual omniscience. In a famous essay Jean-Paul Sartre pilloried François Mauriac for usurping wisdom reserved only to God, who—Sartre concluded with cutting emphasis—is no artist, 'any more than is Mr Mauriac'. As if to forestall precisely this broadside some novelists have followed the example of Flaubert, who in *Madame Bovary* uses omniscience with such discretion that it passes virtually unnoticed, or the example of James, whose narrator in *The Bostonians* roguishly denies possessing full omniscience whenever it suits his purpose to keep the reader in ignorance of the characters' state of mind. Others, again, have followed Dickens's practice in *Bleak House* (intercalating Esther's narrative with omniscient narrative and allowing her occasionally to narrate things not observed by her but reported to her by others), or have imitated the manner in which Conrad in *Under Western Eyes* employs an intelligent first-person narrator who has gained privileged access to the mind of another man through the reading of his private diary or correspondence. And some contemporary experimental novelists like

Alain Robbe-Grillet transcend the issue altogether by their abrupt and even unsignposted shifts from one point of view to another, in line with their systematic undermining of the entire traditional notion of consistency.

The stress on point of view serves to remind us, as Arnold Berleant has remarked, that 'reading a novel is really being told a story'. Narrators are obliged sometimes to go to extraordinary lengths to persuade the reader that they have their information on good authority. In the eighteenth century, we noted, it was common for them to pretend that they had found their material in an old cupboard or a strong-box; the convention of the 'found diary' or the 'unpublished correspondence' was rife. Later narrators needed to have their information supplemented by the implied author, as Marlow's narratives are supplemented by Conrad in several of his works. Marcel Proust, although the most consistent user of the I-narrator in the history of fiction, did not trouble himself over-much with this particular problem. There is a painful description in *Time Regained* of Berma giving a tea-party at which the narrator Marcel is clearly not present. He describes it nonetheless in considerable detail, and we are left to assume that he knows about it only by report; he certainly does not enlighten us about the source of his information.

Narrators also have a tendency to deliver themselves of general statements about life. It has often been noticed that novels tend to contain general statements which can almost be called aphorisms. In *The Princess of Cleves* Monsieur de Nemours has just managed, albeit in veiled terms, to declare his love to Madame de Clèves, who finds she likes what she hears more than she should:

> Madame de Clèves was not slow to grasp the way in which these words could be understood to refer to herself. She felt that she should reply to them and not tolerate their imputation. It also seemed to her that she ought not to understand them, nor show that she applied them to herself. She felt obliged to speak, and yet equally compelled to remain silent. Monsieur de Nemours's words pleased and angered her in equal proportions. She saw in them confirmation of all the Dauphine had led her to suspect. She found something gallant and respectful in them side by side with something bold and all too clearly intelligible . . . The most obscure words of the man one is in love with make one more agitated than the overt declarations of a man one doesn't love. So she remained

without answering, and Monsieur de Nemours would have noticed her silence, from which he would perhaps not have drawn inauspicious conclusions, if Monsieur de Clèves's arrival had not brought the conversation and his visit to an end.

In the middle of this analysis of a woman's confused feelings there is a general aphorism which sums up what has just been said about an individual, and clinches the demonstration: 'the most obscure words of the man one is in love with make one more agitated than the overt declarations of a man one doesn't love'. Even Flaubert, who claimed to detest authorial intrusions in a novel, went in for aphorisms, such as this one in *Madame Bovary:*

> Human speech is like a cracked cauldron on which we beat out tunes to make bears dance when our intention rather is to move the stars to pity.

In taking its distance from personal suffering, the novel often has recourse in this way to general statement. It may go so far as to attempt a seduction of the reader. The implied author in Laclos's *Dangerous Liaisons* carries out an inveiglement of the reader parallel to, if in another dimension from, the physical seduction of the innocent victim which is described in the story. A similar conquest is carried out by Camus who (as we saw in Chapter 3) persuades us in *The Outsider* that a man who has been convicted of first-degree murder is essentially innocent. That fiction can operate in such transcendent ways is one of the reasons for its power to subvert and change, and helps explain why earlier generations, as yet not exposed to the even greater impact of audio-visual media, held it in respect and even fear, prosecuting it for obscenity, libel, indecency or blasphemy whenever (like *Madame Bovary*) it stepped out of line and challenged current attitudes beyond what was felt tolerable. This is because, Berleant writes, 'it relates not a realm of truths but evokes a world of human acts, events, and awareness'; he considers that 'this is not verbal communication; it is verbal communion'.

The distinction between 'communication' and 'communion' is well illustrated by the familiar story in the fourth chapter of John's Gospel of the encounter between Jesus and the Samaritan woman at Jacob's Spring. First of all there are two bracketed asides in the story which are not those of a newspaper-style reporter but of a speaker who is momentarily standing outside the narrative to address the reader direct. Also significant is the dramatic way in which the story is unfolded, building up to the moment of Messianic self-revelation when Jesus tells the Samaritan woman that she is speaking to the fabled prophet she has heard so much about.

Even more striking is the evident delight the narrator takes in recounting the almost teasing banter between Jesus and the woman about the true nature of her marital status. There are further levels of irony—which the reader is expected to pick up and simultaneously to notice that the Samaritan woman does not—in the play on the double meaning (literal and metaphorical) of the words 'water' and 'drink'. The whole passage reveals considerable psychological shrewdness, a feeling for conversation in which one of the parties veils his meaning while the other (for the Samaritan woman is not stupid) gradually picks up the sense. And finally, it is soon noticed that the narrative has a perceptible starkness, urgency and pace about it. This is fiction, of course, in that it is playing on more than one level at once, and assumes a relationship with the reader which is indeed, to use Berleant's terms, 'communion' rather than 'communication'. The reader is being spoken to, even knowingly buttonholed, in the Gospel passage.

To return to my starting point, the conventionality of the novel which occasionally irritates Jacobson is of course far less marked than the conventionality of other artistic forms. Italian grand opera, in which women are depicted as strongly passionate viragos singing in husky modulated accents, is a good deal more stereotyped than the novel at its most rigid. This does not mean that it is less effective: opera is arguably the most potent and emotive art form, apart from the film, that mankind has invented. The more conventional and strictly-regulated the form, the more effective it can be in working upon our emotions; Greek tragedy, another artificial form, bears this out. The sheer bulk of the novel would in any case render convention of that degree quite impossible; the conventions of fiction—and the genre certainly has its conventions—are those which we naturally associate with a looser form. Some readers have always acted as if fables were true, from the young men who committed suicide because of the sorrows of young Werther, to television viewers nowadays who send wreaths and flowers to the programmes which 'kill off' characters in order to write out certain actors or actresses. But as John Fowles declares in *The French Lieutenant's Woman*, 'fiction usually pretends to conform to the reality'; the stress here however is on the word 'pretends': it is a pretence of which both author and reader are continually aware, and indeed engage in a kind of conspiracy to perpetuate. The contemporary novelist is frequently unwilling to maintain this gentleman's agreement. Fowles himself says that we live in the age of Robbe-Grillet and the *nouveau roman*; this newest fictional convention questions most familiar assumptions, and substitutes for certainty the word 'perhaps'. In one of the alternative endings to *The French Lieutenant's Woman* Fowles tells the reader: 'what you must not think is that this is a less plausible ending to their story'. In writing a novel as full of surprises, suspense, mysteries, coincidences and chance meetings as any Victorian novel which it lovingly parodies, Fowles at one and the same time obeys the convention and surreptitiously undermines it.

In the universe of the novel, indeed, normal everyday assumptions have to be suspended; it is a world in which so few people, relatively speaking, are involved that coincidence, especially of contemporaneity or encounter, is a striking and indeed characteristic feature. An impressively large number of great novels exploit coincidence in quite startling fashion: the examples range from *Tom Jones*, *War and Peace*, *Great Expectations*, *Journey to the End of the Night* and *The Great Gatsby* to *Doctor Zhivago*. Although it is true that amazing coincidences can occur in everyday life, they are usually neutral and without significance; for instance, of the many million passengers carried each day in the London underground we may meet face to face an almost forgotten person we knew at school. In real life this is unlikely to lead to more than an exhange of greetings and news. In a novel however it would almost certainly lead to major developments in the plot; fiction relies on limited groups of people adrift in the mass, as in *War and Peace*, the classic novel of the mode. Because the novelist can expect the reader to make acquaintance in his novel with only a limited number of characters (just as in the course of life we meet only a relatively small number of people out of the myriads who inhabit the planet), he is obliged to effect permutations and interlinkings between a limited number of people. This is what we mean by coincidence. It is an artificial device, one which the novel persuades us to accept as arising inevitably from the genre's need to imitate life without having at its disposal the full range and multiplicity of life; thus, in *War and Peace*, people are killed not, as in life, at inappropriate moments, but when the plot requires their disappearance.

An analogous convention governs the deployment of significant detail. In *Madame Bovary* Gustave Flaubert uses carefully selected but telling details to persuade us of the intrinsic truthfulness of the situation he evokes. His description of Emma's wedding, for instance, is crowded with detail, the significance of which later becomes clear: the winding procession, the fiddler leading the way, the adornment of his violin, the way Emma's dress drags on the ground, Rouault's ill-fitting suit, the gluttonous lavishness of the wedding feast, and the elaborate wedding cake; all this illumines and illustrates the world in which Emma will be dissatisfied and unhappy because she has been educated out of the class which can take its pleasures as simply and coarsely as the guests at this traditional rural marriage.

Like detail, dialogue in the novel is especially governed by conventions, as V.S. Pritchett has pointed out. 'None of us can express ourselves well', he writes, 'and yet in any class of society the emotional and thinking potential are more or less the same. We need the artist to speak for us, to give us significance'; which he usually does quite unrealistically. And as a result of the experiments of Edouard Dujardin (in *The Laurels are Cut Down*, 1888) even the thought processes of the mind are subject to a treatment which has its own conventions and its own rhetoric; the famous 'stream of consciousness' which Dujardin inaugurated is not at all spontaneous, but merely another and equally stylized form of discourse. Each fictional world is distinct from any other; each employs a different working logic and is scrutinized by the author from different perceptual assumptions.

But these remain conscious structures. There are inevitably deeper structures at work in every novel; and it is these which tend to fall into types or patterns. Critics of fiction have continually been attracted to patterns, or types as they are more accurately termed. In 1928 Edwin Muir made an early and fairly crude attempt at establishing a typology of the novel in terms of the 'character novel', the 'dramatic novel', and the 'chronicle'. More recently German critics have turned their attention to typologies; Franz Stanzel has attempted a classification of narrative situations, and Saad Elkhadem has typified the novel according to intellectual content, as time-novel, man-novel and event-novel. Another way of discerning patterns is to see the novel in terms of subdivisions of the ancient and traditional genres tragedy, epic and comedy.

II

In comic fiction, for instance, there are two basic types of structure: the first is a loose model derived ultimately from Apuleius, the Roman novelist, and more immediately from Cervantes and the Spanish picaresque. It is a very numerous category, indeed it includes most comic novels ever written, from *The Golden Ass* to *Catch-22*, including such very different specimens as *Tristram Shandy,* or *Confessions of Felix Krull Confidence Man,* or *The Good Soldier Svejk.*

In fact, D.J. Enright's review of a new translation of *Svejk,* the Czech novel left unfinished in 1923 by Jaroslav Hasek, sums up admirably the main characteristics of the mode. Writing in *The Listener* (30 August 1973), Enright starts by suggesting that the novel 'is no doubt too long' and is 'essentially shapeless', obsessed with 'the minutiae of martial unheroism' and a 'preponderance of belly and bowels', but that it 'works cumulatively, in the picaresque mode'. Like the picaresque, too, it shows 'an unflagging fascination for the human scene, a vast acquaintanceship and a reservoir of anecdotes', particularly of tall stories. In line with its archetype, again, *Svejk* goes in liberally for 'explicit authorial moralizing'. But this can be overlooked ('happily sparse, it is not very effective') in the light of the bawdy, the blasphemy, the irreverence about the Emperor, the Nation, the Church, Glory, Self-Sacrifice and Victory ('quite simply, the book, as its vulgar characters would say, shits on all of this') which more truly characterize what Enright, summing up his review, considers a 'rough, vigorous, plebian classic', with its hearty message that what alone counts in this life are 'a full belly, a plump woman in bed, and survival'.

The reader will recognize parallels with much else in comic fiction: the preoccupation with the human gut takes us back to *Gargantua and Pantagruel,* the knockabout to *Don Quixote,* the bawdy to *Tom Jones,* the shapelessness to *Jacques the Fatalist,* and the self-mockery to *Tristram Shandy* (in which, it will be remembered, Sterne portrays himself as Parson Yorick; similarly Hasek, who was dismissed as editor of a journal called *Animal World* for writing about imaginary animals, inserts a tall story into *Svejk* about a volunteer called Marek who used to be editor of the same *Animal World* and, 'wishing to offer his readers something new, invented such creatures as the Artful Prosperian'). A character likewise 'gets the job of writing the battalion's history, which he does in advance, reading out to his comrades his stirring accounts of their heroic deaths in action'. This both looks back to *Don Quixote* and

the burlesque intermingling of life with fiction that is characteristic of
the later sections of the novel, where Don Quixote discusses with
Sancho the book in which they both appear; and it looks forward to
Catch-22 in its macabre, even ghoulish preoccupation with morbidity
and death.

Indeed, Enright wonders whether Catch-22 is not the 'child of Svejk';
he might well have added that Svejk's father is Grimmelshausen's
classic story of the Thirty Years' War, Simplicius Simplicissimus (1669),
which tempers much bawdy and belly-filling with philosophical
discussion, with an account of a fantastic journey to the centre of the
earth, with religious considerations that run through the comedy in the
manner of The Golden Ass (which is also under its burlesque frolics a
mystical work), and with a tale of mystery and suspense after the
manner of Dickens (in that the secret of Simplicius's noble birth is
revealed only near the end). It is characteristic of this unconcentrated
kind of fiction that it should shoot off rather wildly at several targets at
once; consistency is the very least of its concerns.

One of the great comic novels in the English language, Pickwick
Papers, illustrates this point rather well. The characterization is on the
Cervantes model: the central character, Mr Pickwick, is supplied with
a servant who contrasts strongly with him, Sam Weller; and as Don
Quixote transcended the parody of romance which was its point of
departure, Dickens's text gradually adopted a more ambitious scope as
it developed from its origin as an accompaniment to sporting sketches.
The concept which launched the book changed as the guiding
principles were modified: the Pickwick Club is progressively lost sight
of, and only picked up again at the end to round off the story and
ensure that it is all well and truly done with (a precaution Cervantes
takes also, by restoring Quixote to sanity and then killing him safely
off). The basic structure is Cervantesque, too, in that Pickwick Papers
consists of adventures interlarded with anecdotes recounted by people
met with on the road. At the centre of the novel stands Pickwick
himself, a good if impetuous man who, like Quixote, mellows slowly;
but for all his blunders Pickwick, unlike Quixote, is a force for good. In
this respect the novel is more optimistic than Cervantes's, and indeed
all turns out right at the end of the rather contrived plot. The realism
without illusions which characterizes Don Quixote, suggesting that only
when idealism is dead and drab normality is restored can all be said to
be well again, contrasts strongly with Pickwick's buoyant nineteenth-
century optimism that the good shall triumph, the wicked will be

vanquished, the transgressor like Alfred Jingle will reform and all will live in peace, virtue and harmony ever after.

Proust, too, though not usually thought of as a great comic writer, offers much in *Remembrance of Things Past* which is comic, even Dickensian, in inspiration. Social satire was Proust's strong point, such as that of the social climber and arch-snob, Madame Verdurin, who will have her literary *salon* even if it means ruling the *habitués* with an iron hand, ruthlessly persecuting the slack and faint-hearted, and accepting social nonentities provided they obey the rules. And the way Proust progressively destroys his characters or introduces abrupt changes into their circumstances makes over the whole span of his novel a comic point in itself.

There is, however, a much tighter form of comic fiction, in which the virtuosity lies in the very neatness with which the ends are tied up. The classic instance is *Tom Jones,* which was first praised for the perfection of its plot by Coleridge, and more recently by the Chicago critic R.S. Crane in an influential essay ('The Concept of Plot and the Plot of *Tom Jones*'). But almost as neat is the structure of Joyce's *Ulysses* (in the close co-ordinates it establishes with the *Odyssey*) and of Evelyn Waugh's first novel *Decline and Fall,* with its tart satirical effects deriving in large measure from the artful circularity of a story which begins and ends with Pennyfeather at Oxford. In the first chapter he is innocently involved in undergraduate rowdyism and sent down; in the last, older, wiser, with the same name but an assumed identity, he is careful not to launch himself and the novel on the threatened wild *da capo*. There are understandably fewer works in this tighter comic category: and equally understandably, the sub-genre is most in evidence in the modernist period. One of the greatest of all examples of the mode is Samuel Beckett's novel of 1938, *Murphy*.

Many of *Murphy's* features derive from the broad tradition of the comic novel: a convoluted style (the baroque conversation *à trois* between Neary, Wylie and Miss Counihan for example), a way with words ('genustuprations'—a form of what is more vulgarly known as footsy-footsy—is only one of several witty coinings), and a penchant for ironic communion with the reader ('this phrase is chosen with care, lest the filthy censors should lack an occasion to commit their filthy synecdoche', confides Beckett in a characteristic knock at the theocracy of his native land). Like most other comic novels, too, *Murphy* is not a particularly gentle book: it is cruel towards many of its butts, not least the small shopkeeper, whose wife is sharply characterized as a 'semi-private convenience' and his son as its principal 'waste product'.

But the main interest of *Murphy* in the present context is its plot. The novel is a joke in its very form—a learned joke at its own expense—as can be seen in the intricate analogies Beckett establishes between his story and the star-charts and almanacs for the year 1935 in which the main events take place. The various elements of the plot are carefully interlocked; the chronology is shuffled while still remaining coherent; and the story is at once intricately flawless and ludicrously improbable, in that the entire plot hinges on the implausible multiple pursuit of Murphy. Beckett sustains too a parody of such forms of fiction as the thriller (Chapter 5 ends on a note of high suspense) and the lending library romance (Celia the golden-hearted whore is almost redeemed by true love before cruel fate intervenes; potential tragedy however is deftly undercut in the burlesque scene in the mortuary, when the doctor and the coroner bandy witticisms across Murphy's corpse). This cool macabre is characteristic of the greatest comic novels, such as Gogol's *Dead Souls* (in which the hero goes about 'buying up' deceased serfs). The novel is, moreover, full of quips in the best comic tradition: from literary puns like 'night's young thoughts' to bawdy innuendo about how Celia and Murphy can both 'manage' in a narrow bed. But as I said earlier the joking is not only at that level: it is also at the level of the whole book. The novel itself is a joke at its own expense, a dour joke no doubt, but a resounding joke for all that, the best laugh of the lot residing in the fact that the work is a parody of itself, a circular book-about-nothing such as Flaubert dreamed of, in which Murphy's misadventures are the preposterously unreal pretext for constructing a fabric of fiction which will stand by itself, slender, delicate, elegant, and yet sadly gratuitous.

The comic attitude to life, it is clear, rests upon dissociation: the reader is deliberately distanced. Pain and suffering, even Murphy's ('all the puppets in this book whinge sooner or later', the narrator tells us, 'except Murphy, who is not a puppet') are curiously anaesthetized, robbed of their meaning, and the reader is not permitted to become too closely involved with the serious implications (even in an uneasily message-ridden book like *Catch-22*). So much so that the relationship between humour and dissociation becomes the serious part of laughter: the world is distanced because it is too horrific, and the comic is held up as the only means of withstanding the onslaught of so much misery, and as a protection for our sensibilities. There is clearly a mode in which comedy—whether its structure is tight or loose—can become the most serious of all art forms: because unhappiness, as Beckett says through one of the characters in his play *Endgame*, is the funniest thing in the world; how otherwise, one pertinently wonders, could man have learned to bear it?

III

So much, in a general way, for deep structures discernable in the novel. We may, finally, legitimately ask ourselves what it is that makes great fiction, as opposed to the second-rate. Certainly not pretensions: American 'blockbusters' are strikingly pretentious, either in prominently listing the research and documentation which went into their creation, even going so far as to specify the university library where the material (plus the MS drafts) is deposited, as in Irving Stone's *The Agony and the Ecstasy*; or they reveal their pretensions by their 'sophisticated' construction: in Harold Robbins's *79 Park Avenue*, for example, first-person narrative using swift flashback is interwoven with third-person narration employing linear chronology in a more leisurely form. Also leitmotifs, admittedly of an obvious kind, can be discerned even in second or third rate fiction. A detective story, although constructed on highly artificial lines from the *dénouement* backwards so that a striking (but in retrospect obvious) opening can be presented, may reveal a consciousness of evil and of destiny which gives it an extra dimension; as I argued in Chapter 5, this is the case with Simenon.

Science fiction is similarly a capacious and uneven category of popular fiction. The first serious survey I am aware of—*New Maps of Hell* by Kingsley Amis (1961)—has considerable difficulty in defining it. Cohabiting uneasily with fantasy writing on the one hand and the crazier forms of prophecy on the other, it is, Amis says, 'every day losing some of its appropriateness',as *science* fiction—in other words, the gadgetry side of it is becoming less and less important. At its purest, Amis claims, it 'presents with verisimilitude the human effects of spectacular changes in our environment, changes either deliberately willed or involuntarily suffered'. The more 'optimistic' sort of story tends to study willed, even desirable changes; the more 'pessimistic'—and to my mind by far the more interesting and significant—deals with developments beyond human control and volition and concentrates on their destructive effects. The common ancestor of books of this latter type—the kind written by two of the leading current practitioners of the art, J.G. Ballard and Christopher Priest—is none other than that (incongruous) classic of our children's bookshelves, *Gulliver's Travels*. As Erich Kahler has written:

> The third part of *Gulliver's Travels*, with its descriptions of a miscellany of island peoples, has generally been viewed as an inessential, weaker insertion into the book. To my mind this view is very wrong. The section adds a horizontal dimension to the vertical dimensions in which human limits are exceeded in the other parts. Here Swift selects professional abilities and individual functions out of the human totality and shows how each of these can degenerate. He explores the potentialities of reaching beyond ordinary human lifetimes and human ways, into immortality, to the ghosts of history. This part is, in fact, the most contemporary part of the book for us. It contains astonishing prophecies of some of the most recent experimentation, and of the quantitative approach that is dominant nowadays. There is, first of all, the flying island of Laputa, a kind of satellite on which dwell the mathematicians who rule the common folk on the land beneath.
>
> *The Inward Turn of Narrative*, pp. 123-4

Swift, Kahler argues, used the new modes of perception inaugurated by the era of scientific discovery to reveal in a prophetic fashion the dehumanizing possibilities of science itself; and it is clear that the finest science fiction writers today are not attempting anything very different. The father of an illustrious line, Swift remains, Kahler concludes, 'the earliest and at the same time the most radical of the "cultural pessimists" ' (p. 130). Amis also links modern science fiction to *Gulliver's Travels*, which he praises for its verisimilitude and eschewal of the arbitrary, for its 'businesslike thoroughness in description [of] a series of satirical utopias' (p. 31).

The feature of science fiction which Amis stresses—and which connects it so firmly with *Gulliver's Travels*, and then later with Voltaire's *Micromégas* (1752), the first account of a visit to Earth by an alien, and with Samuel Butler's *Erewhon* (1872), a satirical romance in which names are spelt backwards and common notions like the value of machinery or the appropriateness of legal punishment for theft are set on their heads—the feature science fiction has in common with such works is what Amis calls 'social diagnosis and warning', a 'didactic and amonitory purpose'. 'Its most important use', he writes, 'is a means of dramatizing social enquiry, as providing a fictional mode in which cultural tendencies can be isolated and judged' (p. 63). While trying first and foremost to entertain, science fiction writers are concerned secondarily to warn us of the dangers of our technology or of the potential hazards of the apparently 'safe' world we inhabit. Thus J.G. Ballard compares familiar Shaftesbury Avenue and Holborn in London to 'a city of hell' after it has been torn to pieces by freak winds of a strength previously experienced only by those employed to simulate aircraft slipstreams in wind-tunnels (see *The Wind from Nowhere*, 1962). In Ballard's later novel, *The Drought* (1965), rain is a thing of the past because radio-active waste has prevented the sea evaporating, with consequences which can be imagined: a perverted new type of human being is bred out of the dead land, bitter and murderous, and traditional values are turned upside down; water replaces money and like it becomes the source of a new evil. The opposite disaster afflicts the people of *The Drowned World* (1962), also by Ballard; and in John Christopher's *The Death of Grass* (published in the United States as *No Blade of Grass*) all civilized qualities are overturned when a mutating virus attacks all seed-bearing herbage and robs man of his daily bread in a 'silent spring' beyond even Rachel Carson's worst imagining.

'It is a curious paradox' (writes Ballard in the preface to *Vermilion Sands*, 1973) 'that almost all science fiction, however far removed in time and space, is really about the present day . . . Perhaps because of [its] cautionary tone, so much of science fiction's notional futures are zones of unrelieved grimness. Even its heavens are like other people's hells'. This is not always true: there is, as I said earlier, a more optimistic vein in some science fiction, perhaps best represented by one of the classics of the genre, Isaac Asimov's *Foundation Trilogy* (1951-53), in which against great odds and in spite of near-disaster the best of mankind's achievement survives the collapse into decadent barbarism of the First Empire and the galaxy is finally made 'safe for ever'. Some science fiction on the other hand involves puzzles or paradoxes, a kind of black surrealist humour such as marks Christopher Priest's first novel *Indoctrinaire* (1970) and his third, *Inverted World* (1974), both of which are concerned with distortions of time or space. *Indoctrinaire* tells how a circular clearing of stubble in the middle of the Brazilian jungle exists two hundred years in the future: in moving out of the trees on to this plain the characters step across two centuries of time. British scientist Elias Wentik is drafted there in mysterious circumstances; when he returns to England it is to find it in the middle of a war and his family evacuated from London he knows not where. In despair he awaits the impending nuclear holocaust, since in spite of everything he decides not to go back (or rather perhaps forward) to the safety of the future.

Inverted World, though Priest's third novel, had been 'simmering' in his mind since 1965 and has more in common with *Indoctrinaire* than it has with his second and to my mind his finest book *Fugue for a Darkening Island* (1972). The 'inverted world' of the title is Earth City. To its inhabitants it is an oasis of peace, order and civilized values, built on another planet by an enlightened visionary when Earth itself was engulfed in disaster and barbarism (this is of course a recurrent theme in science fiction). It is a place where the physical laws governing Earth are inverted 'we live', one of the inhabitants declares, 'in a large but finite universe, occupied by a number of bodies of infinite size' (N.E.L. ed., p. 178). This picture which they have of their world is cast in doubt by the attitude of an intelligent outsider, an English nurse called Elizabeth Khan, to whom the City appears to be 'not much more than a large and misshapen office block' (p. 221). Their world-view is finally shattered when it becomes clear that it is not the exterior world that is different, but their perception of it. Imprisoned in their inherited and unquestioned beliefs, they have for ages been laboriously winching their 'city' forward on rails in a continually-frustrated attempt to maintain it near the elusive 'optimum' where they claim spatial and temporal distortion is at its minimum. It comes almost as much of a shock to the reader to realize that they have been dragging themselves across Spain and Portugal in a post-'Crash' world and, having reached the western seaboard of the European land-mass, are about to haul themselves into the endless stretches of the Atlantic. The alternative world-view they have lived by for so long turns out to have been a mere mathematical abstraction based on a hyperbolic curve, and they are saved only in the nick of time from the suicidal consequences of believing in it any longer.

In spite of its rather unsatisfying 'trick' ending, *Inverted World* is not without disturbing features which link it with the satirical utopias of earlier literature. I am not thinking of the rather too blatant parallel with the myth of the expulsion from the Garden of Eden when the hero-narrator Helward Mann yields to the temptation of a latter-day Eve called Caterina bearing apples, or of a perhaps coincidental similarity with *Erewhon* (in which wealth is measured in horsepower just as in Earth City age is computed in miles). I am referring to the technique of ironic contrast—set up between an imaginary or ideal world and our own—which is the staple of Swiftean or Voltairean satire and is not lost even on the hero himself:

> Perhaps unfairly, I formed an impression that I should not care to live on Earth planet, as most of its existence seemed to be a series of disputes, wars, territorial claims, economic pressures. The concept of civilization was far advanced, and explained to us as the state in which mankind congregated within cities. By definition, we of Earth city were civilized, but there seemed to be no resemblance between our existence and theirs. Civilization on Earth planet was equated with selfishness and greed; those people who lived in a civilized state exploited those who did not. There were shortages of vital commodities on Earth planet, and the people in the civilized nations were able to monopolize those commodities by reason of their greater economic strength. This imbalance appeared to be at the root of the disputes.
>
> I suddenly saw parallels between our civilization and theirs. The city was undoubtedly on a war footing as a result of the situation with the tooks, and that in its turn was a product of our barter system. We did not exploit them through wealth, but we had a surplus of the commodities in short supply on Earth planet: food, fuel energy, raw materials. Our shortage was manpower, and we paid for that with our surplus commodities.
>
> The process was inverted, but the product was the same.
>
> N.E.L. ed., pp. 166-67

The thrust of that last sentence is reminiscent of many of Swift's best effects when he unveils his meaning directly after an extended development of oblique and dead-pan treatment.

I have already suggested that Priest's finest novel is *Fugue for a Darkening Island*. Perhaps it is no coincidence that this is more 'prophetic' (in the Orwellian sense at least) than either of the other two, and less like classic science fiction. It is described by its publishers variously as 'imaginative fiction' and as 'a novel of the future'. This future, like that of *Nineteen Eighty-Four*, is not especially remote, in fact it is uncomfortably close to home. The 'darkening island' is of course Britain; more particularly, the south-east of England in which the entire action is played out. A nuclear holocaust in Africa has driven millions of blacks to seek refuge elsewhere, and many thousands land illegally in England, provoking racial tension on a scale hitherto unknown. A right-wing government attempts to impose a tough policy of control, opposed by liberal elements (among which the hero Alan Whitman numbers himself). The Africans take up arms to defend themselves; the whites react in kind. Law and order breaks down; atrocity and counter-atrocity disfigure communal life. Alan Whitman—the epitome of the ordinary man-in-the-street, a modest college lecturer unhappily married with a young daughter—is not much better at coping with this situation than most of his compatriots; perhaps less so, in that he is a moral and physical coward who has opted out all his life from difficult political, personal and moral decisions. He is the sort of man who having seduced a girl blames the sexual failure of their subsequent marriage on her, and takes up with a string of mistresses with whom he is scarcely less indifferent. His only deep relationship is with his daughter Sally: he stays with his wife only on her account. His personal slide into barbarism is precipitated by the one occurrence which can provoke in him a 'combination of terror and hatred': the discovery of Sally's mutilated body near a brothel set up by the blacks for their troops, one of many female victims who have been murdered for failing to 'co-operate'.

This is thus a much more unsettling novel than Priest's other books It is also more insistently and disturbingly erotic: the other two, like much science fiction, are perfunctory in their treatment of sex. There is, too, an uneasy tension between liberal attitudes on the one hand and deep-seated anxieties about racial conflict on the other: if *Inverted World* features 'tooks', primitive people whom the City exploits with the good conscience Helward comes to see through in the passage I quoted above, it does not betray fear of them in the way *Fugue* does. What I am saying is that Priest's second novel appears less 'censored' by his own enlightened feelings than the other two; and for that reason it is a more honest, more disturbing and altogether more satisfying book. I do not of course imply for a moment that it deserves that ugly contemporary epithet 'racist': just that it is too clear-sighted to suppress the fact that white people in the situation of a 'darkening island' would oppose mass black immigration, that the blacks would resist measures to expel them, and that if nothing were done to defuse the confrontation the consequences for all parties to the dispute would be ugly and cruel. What Priest is writing about, in a word, is what Ingmar Bergman in one of his greatest films refers to as 'the shame' (in fact the movie may have inspired the book: the imagery of the end is very similar in both cases, the refugee boat, the shapeless bodies in the sea, and so on): the shame anyone would experience in a situation of social breakdown for which he would necessarily feel obscurely responsible.

Fugue is also the most interesting technically of Priest's novels. It is written from several temporal viewpoints: Alan's boyhood and precocious sexual experiences, his student days and developing relationship with his future wife, his married life and various mistresses, the worsening political situation as the African problem grows in menace, the different stages of the breakdown of normal British life; all these moments in time are visited in turn but in no particular order. As in many *nouveaux romans*, the reader is expected to find his own bearings from internal indications; none of the individual sections of narrative extends for more than a few pages. The style, too, resembles the impersonal, inexplicit manner familiar in French experimental writing.

But much as it owes to other contemporary fiction, *Fugue for a Darkening Island* is a genuinely original work of art. It is science fiction only in the broadest sense of the term; like the best of the genre, it transcends simple definitions. At the same time it is comfortably at home in a long tradition of moral and didactic fiction, playing utopia (in this case the town on the south coast, an unnatural oasis of order and calm in a world of chaos, which offers Whitman shelter for a time) against the horrors of reality. A reality that if not contemporary is not unthinkable either; it is clear that Priest's consciousness, like that of the rest of his generation—he was born in England two years before Hiroshima—is seared by an awareness of the hydrogen bomb, which casts its shadow not only over the 'darkening island' but also over the world of *Indoctrinaire*. 'It is one thing to imagine an atrocity', Whitman confides, 'it is something else again to witness it' (pp. 84-85); for, as Robert Jay Lifton has pointed out, 'we are all survivors of Hiroshima simply by living in a world in which the bomb was dropped'. If one of the functions of literature is to remind and warn, Christopher Priest's work fulfills it powerfully. Like Artaud in the theatre, Priest no doubt sees his task as being to alert us that we are not free, since the heavens may at any time fall about our ears.

In general, however, would-be seriousness, let alone documentation, construction and leitmotifs are not by themselves enough to distinguish between the excellent in fiction and the moderately competent, not to mention all the degrees in between. What distinguishes the second-rate lies elsewhere. Such novels are poorly written; by this is meant that the style is drab and does not work for the book. The characterization is elementary (the figures are like cardboard cut-outs, casting no shadow). Consequently any mystery in the character (as in the heroine of *79 Park Avenue*) is not a deliberate mystery created by contrast with the less mysterious, but one due to the inability of the author to do more than simply say, 'she was mysterious'. The sentiments in such books are tawdry: the erotic slips into the pornographic, and the moving into the sentimental, since the author is incapable of keeping the balance. There is a lack of overall, consistent inspiration; the second-rate may be superficially more competent, tying up loose ends and so on, but it is profoundly incompetent in that it gives no impression of having sprung from a coherent vision.

All this applies not to the obvious rubbish and near-pornography that litters our bookstalls, but rather to the rubbishy near-pornography which takes itself seriously, which sets out to be 'art'. It is this sort of writing which John Carey demolished deftly and effectively in a review of Leslie Thomas's novels. Thomas is the author of *The Virgin Soldiers* and other best-sellers, and this is how Carey concluded his very necessary hatchet-job:

Sorting out what makes readers go for this particular kind of fantasy is apt to look heavy-footed, and best left to psychologists. But a puritanical sense that adult sexuality is shameful or sullied arguably lies behind the recurrent need for child's play. The toys and prattle of Mr Thomas's mini-bedmates are designed to suggest pristine innocence (an innocence which combines, as it cannot in life, with sexual expertise). *The Love Beach*, for instance, has a would-be Edenic scene in which some 11-year-old girls perform an erotic dance, 'laughing the laughter of innocence and childishness', watched by the gloating hero. A muddled desire to restore innocence may explain, too, the primness with which sexual deviations are treated in the novels, once they have been amply catered for. In *The Man with the Power* a prostitute gives Willy a stirring account of a whipping she has received from a client. Afterwards Willy has a deep sense of shame at his 'horrible, sick' feelings, and it transpires that the woman made up the whole story, simulating the weals with cosmetics. So the novel cleanses itself, as it were, of the pollution it has fostered. The underlying guilt and shame plainly connect with the prevalent boyishness elsewhere. The underlying fear, too. What the novels shrink from is the idea of having sex with a woman who is the man's equal (or superior) in maturity and intellect.

The Listener, 22 November 1973

We instinctively know this sort of writing to be second-rate, but cannot always say why as incisively as Carey does. It is not a matter of structure, leitmotif, and so on, as I have shown. It is more a matter of depth, or simply of integrity and coherence of vision. 'Sincerity' is no guide because there is little doubt that Robbins, Stone, Thomas and the rest are 'sincere', even touchingly so, in their attempts to write honestly and well. The sincerity of the artist, however, lies not in his motives but in his achievement, his results. Stendhal, alias Beyle, was in many ways a deceitful man and writer, but one of the most honest of novelists: his honesty lay in the consistency and clarity of his inspiration. The other kind of novel is, after all, a marketed *product*: fidelity is expected of the consumer to the product. Erle Stanley Gardner's Perry Mason books clearly expect the reader to recognize the characters such as Perry himself and District Attorney Hamilton Burger, and to anticipate the standard formula imbroglio/courtroom scene/solution. In such fiction the characters remain constant from book to book even though the plot may vary in circumstantial details. This harks back to the multi-volume romances of the seventeenth century, of which the archetype is *L'Astrée* (1607-1628), and later on to the serials of nineteenth-century fiction. For such novelists are to some extent pedagogues: Gardner's description in *The Case of the Fan-Dancer's Horse* of the shadow-box, a sort of sophisticated identification parade system, could be paralleled by many an 'instructive' passage in Balzac. The form has changed little in the interval, except to degenerate into the sclerosis of artificiality.

There are, in fact, certain basic patterns in fiction, such as in the nineteenth century the adultery theme, or the motif of the son and heir falling into the clutches of a *femme fatale,* described ironically in *Madame Bovary* as 'that eternal bugbear of families, the vague pernicious creature, the siren, the monster which dwells fantastically in the deep places of love'. Such patterns or structures come to be expected by the reader and voluntarily accepted. Thus in a detective story it is usually one of the least conspicuous characters who turns out to be the criminal, and indications which no one else would notice provide the sleuth with the key to the mystery ('elementary, my dear Watson'); originality lies in variation upon the standard schema, while remaining within the general convention. The reader cooperates with the author by accepting these conventions; without this cooperation no fiction, however trivial, can work. Although popular forms of the novel do not investigate vital areas of human consciousness and experience as do the works I have concentrated on in this study, they sometimes have a strength and sureness of technique which entertains and instructs at the level of the common man, and so should not automatically be disdained. Occasionally a character in popular fiction (Sherlock Holmes is a good example) can attain mythical stature; and even at their worst bestsellers do at least—as Claud Cockburn has reminded us—'produce a good grade of opium'. A fitting way to keep things in proper perspective might be to adapt words Denis Brogan applied to historical studies: 'we can read and should read literature, great and small, in part to feed our imaginations with a sense of the tragic in human life'; especially if, by the 'tragic', we understand whatever enhances our awareness, and enriches our experience, of the world we live in—as fiction truly does.

BIBLIOGRAPHY:
General Studies of the Novels Mentioned in the Text

BOOTH, Wayne C. *The Rhetoric of Fiction*, University of Chicago Press, 1961.

BRERETON, Geoffrey. *A Short History of French Literature*, Penguin, 1954.

COCKBURN, Claud. *Bestseller: The Books that Everyone Read 1900-1939*, Sidgwick & Jackson, 1972.

DUPONT, Victor. *Cinq Leçons de littérature anglaise*, Faculté des Lettres de Toulouse, 1968.

DYSON, A.E. *Between Two Worlds*, Macmillan, 1972.

ELKHADEM, Saad. *Zur Geschichte des deutschen Romans*, Herbert Lang, 1973.

KAHLER, Erich. *The Inward Turn of Narrative*, Princeton University Press, 1973.

KERMODE, Frank. *The Sense of an Ending*, Oxford University Press, 1967.

LEAVIS, F.R. *The Great Tradition: George Eliot, Henry James, Joseph Conrad*, Chatto & Windus, 2nd ed. 1960.

LEVIN, Harry. *The Gates of Horn: A Study of Five French Realists*, Oxford University Press, 1963.

MAYOUX, Jean-Jacques. *L'Humour et l'absurde: Attitudes anglo-saxonnes, attitudes françaises*, Clarendon Press, 1973.

MUIR, Edwin. *The Structure of the Novel*, Hogarth Press, 1928.

ROBBE-GRILLET, Alain. *Snapshots and Towards a New Novel* Calder & Boyars, 1965.

STANZEL, Franz. *Narrative Situations in the Novel: Tom Jones, Moby Dick, The Ambassodors, Ulysses*, Indiana University Press, 1971.

TRILLING, Lionel. *The Liberal Imagination: Essays on Literature and Society*, Viking Press, 1950.

188

WAGNER, Geoffrey. *Five for Freedom: A Study of Feminism in Fiction*, Allen & Unwin, 1972.
WATT, Ian. *The Rise of the Novel: Studies in Defoe, Richardson, and Fielding*, Chatto & Windus, 1957.
ZIOLKOWSKI, Theodore. *Fictional Transfigurations of Jesus*, Princeton University Press, 1972.

190